How Running Saves Lives

The Story of Dickie Longo: A Man for Our Times as Told by Sue Oaks

BY DICKIE LONGO

DORRANCE
PUBLISHING CO
EST. 1920
PITTSBURGH, PENNSYLVANIA 15238

Dorrance Publishing Co
585 Alpha Drive
Pittsburgh, PA 15238
Visit our website at *www.dorrancebookstore.com*

ISBN: 978-1-6386-7057-5
ESIBN: 978-1-6386-7879-3

Table of Contents

Introduction

Dickie Longo has a huge impact on the people around him, but remains humble, friendly, and extremely likeable! He is a cherished husband of sixty-one years, a much-loved father, grandfather, and great-grandfather and a valued long-term employee. He is a loved brother, a loyal parishioner, and a friend to many. But it is the broader impact of which I would like to write—that of his small acts of kindness and his inspiration to many in the field of running, a sport in which he has a physical and online presence that has spanned the globe, and through which he continues to inspire people, at his senior age of eighty-four—though age is but a number! It was this inspirational storytellingthat gave me an insatiable urge to help him get his story down in a more permanent way, and so became the book you are now reading.

Dickie has been keeping a Facebook page since 2017, and it has grown from small posts describing the races he was looking forward to, to posts that have the intention of motivating and inspiring others by relating his many acts of kindness to the needy in the community and sharing his own weekly adventures in various 5k races across America, and encouraging people from all walks of life to pick up a pair of sneakers and try out the sport. It is here that I first heard of him, on a Facebook page dedicated to those who love to run.

After following his posts for a while, I decided to reach out to him personally, for my curiosity had been ignited. What drove this man, I wondered, to be so kind and giving, and to share his life story on the internet? Why did I feel so inspired to keep on running—despite my lack of talent in the field—just by reading his posts? What motivated Dickie to keep racing in 5k races, week after week, and always with a big smile on his face at the end? For while many people like running, no one is like this man—and I wanted to know more.

And so began my exploration. The more I found out about Dickie, the more I was curious. The challenges of his early childhood that may have led another person with a different makeup to go downhill, and choose all sorts of unhealthy coping methods, have contributed instead, I believe, to Dickie's strong character. He demonstrates resilience, strength, stamina, and a drive to succeed that are all underscored by a love of others and a generosity of spirit. While Dickie's relationship with his mother was taken from him prematurely, his father provided a home and upbringing that was more than adequate, despite the scant resources of the post-WWII era. Was it this childhood experience that flowed through his veins, building Dickie's infallible drive to succeed against adversity? Was that what ignited his passion, one which drives his need to continue training and racing, week after week? Did his relationship with his father contribute to his inner drive to provide for the community throughout his athletic and coaching career?

And then, the more I found out about Dickie, the more he remained a mystery. For what inspires a man in his eighties to continue working faithfully as a publishing sales rep, to enable him to give free shoes and clothing to those in need and to fund his scholarship for runners who need financial assistance? What helps him conquer the fear of coronavirus, as the world goes into lockdown? What ignites his desire to continue to inspire and motivate others with his kindness, despite the obvious risk to his own health and life?

There are factors that drive his passion, including his burning love for his wife Beverley and for God, and he has faithfully served his family, church, and community with persistence and perseverance, touching all who know him with his kindness and enthusiasm. This book will explore what drives the man, and hopefully inspire you to reach for the best version of yourself that you can become—in running, in sport, and in life.

CHAPTER ONE

Dickie Longo –
Whose life was saved by running

Dickie has many acts of kindness to his name, and this book will no doubt only touch on a few examples, while many others will remain a secret to just Dickie and those who received them—for despite Dickie's openness about his kindness to others, he is at heart extremely humble. But each act of kindness that we do know about highlights Dickie's sense of social justice and his desire to help those in need, and each one is an inspiration to others. His acts of kindness have no doubt also encouraged the receiver in ways we may never know.

When Dickie retired at the age of sixty-five, (at the time of writing, Dickie is eighty-four years of age), he received a "really good" retirement package. But his retirement lasted two months. Wanting to stay active, he returned to work and he now has two jobs and works five days a week. The money he makes goes towards his Longo Scholarship Fund, buying shoes for runners, running outfits, entry fees, educational expenses for runners and other things that runners need.

"This is my way of giving back to how much running has done for me," he wrote. "It saved my life as a nine-year old."

What follows in the next chapter, are some examples of Dickie's kindness.

In September 2019, Dickie went to the parish county football stadium, to run his four-hundred-meter intervals to get ready for the Miracle Mile race. On finishing his training, he noticed a boy of about fifteen years of age, sitting on the steps, and asked him if he was a runner. He replied, "sort of" and explained that his running shoes had worn out and he could not get new ones as he had no money. Dickie offered his own shoes to the boy, (and his phone number to call if he needed new shoes or anything else). The boy was so grateful for the shoes that he immediately went out and started running, and Dickie drove home in his socks.

The next day, Dickie went to City Park Oval to run and saw two young men sitting on the bench. He handed them a pair of running shorts and shirts and told them to go and change in the locker room. One of the boys said he couldn't run much because he had asthma, and Dickie told him to run what he could because running can cure asthma. They ran together and Dickie said, "Let's finish strong," and the boy ran off and finished way ahead of Dickie. The other boy offered to give Dickie's shoes back, but Dickie said they could keep them and the running outfits and gave them both twenty dollars. One of the boys was a dishwasher at a restaurant and he told Dickie that he was living with his aunt, and his brother was in jail. Dickie encouraged this boy to enroll in 2nd semester for junior college and that he would co-sign for a student loan and pay it off if he could not. The boy went home to share his good news with his aunt.

In October 2019, Dickie was at a race and was sitting on a bench next to a mother and her son. There were a lot of kids there and the race was sponsored by a school. Dickie overheard the child saying that he did not want to run the race without his granddad, and his mother replying, "he would want you to." Dickie asked if he could be of help and the child's mother explained that the boy's granddad had recently died. Filled with compassion, Dickie offered to take the child's granddad's place and run the race with him, and the boy took up the offer. They ran together, and Dickie noticed that the boy was wearing gym shoes, and not runners. After the race, he asked the child's mother to email their address and the boy's shoe size. He sent him a new pair of running shoes and a free subscription to the *Runner's World* magazine. In the shoebox, Dickie tucked in a note that said, "Next year we will run together, but you will need to practice so we can win." The boy's mother later sent him a message by email that touched his heart—she was extremely grateful.

Dickie went to a park to do a hill run that he does regularly, a three-mile grass route with six hills. He was running when about eight high school boys passed him, and he saw it was a boy who lived nearby, who he had seen running in the neighborhood. After both of their training had finished, Dickie introduced himself, and as they chatted, he glanced at the boy's shoes and noticed they were in bad shape. Apparently, the coach had found them in the locker room last year, and given them to the boy, and they were almost worn out. Finding out his shoe size, Dickie went to the running shoe store and asked for the best cross-country shoe they had, in the right size and he was able to negotiate a slightly better price. Not long after, Dickie ran to the boy's home with the shoebox under his arm and dropped the box at the doorstep. At his next cross-country meet, Dickie asked him how he went, and he replied that he had a good result. He smiled shyly, and said, "Thanks for the shoes, Mr. Longo."

Dickie attends a small church and has sat in the same seat for fifty-one years. In front of him sits a lady who has sat in the same seat for about forty years. She is aware that he is a runner, and once told him that her son, in the military, was being deployed for a year and his wife and six children were staying with her at her house, five girls and one boy. She told him that the boy tried out for the cross-country team and made it as a freshman, and she wanted Dickie to talk to him about running and help him. Dickie did exactly that, chatted to the boy and gave some advice. He called the boy's grandmother and asked what kind of shoes he had, and she told him they were only tennis shoes. Dickie went to the running shoe store and bought a good pair, then dropped them at his school, requesting he gets the shoes by 2:00 P.M. because he runs a race at 3:00 P.M. In the box, he left a note, "Good luck and run hard." Later, Dickie received a thank-you card from him, which read:

"Mr. Longo, thank you for the shoes. I like them a lot. We won the race, and I ran 3rd on our team. Signed, 'Your friend.'"

One of Dickie's friends of forty years became a widow when her husband died of a heart attack. She was shocked to find that he did not have a funeral policy and could not afford the funeral expenses. Dickie offered to help with the expenses and gave her a check for $700.00 and a pair of running shoes for his grandson. He told him that his grandfather's heart was weak because he never exercised or ran and asked him to start a running program to strengthen his heart.

In November 2019, Dickie was waiting for the awards to be given out after a race. The 80+ age group is always the last one to be awarded, and by this time, most people had left. Dickie went to his car and found his battery was dead. After calling AAA Road Service, a nice young mechanic arrived to install a new battery. Dickie noticed he looked trim and asked if he was a runner, and he said he did like to run. He did not attend races, though, due to the cost. Dickie noticed he was wearing a pair of old basketball shoes, which he said he ran in and he offered to have a race with him. Dickie took a pair of slightly used running shoes from the car and two twenty-dollar bills, and told the mechanic to use the money for his entry fee and to wear the running shoes, and he will see him in two weeks and run the race together.

In December 2019, Dickie stopped at an intersection on the way to practice his 5k run at a park. There he found a homeless man sitting on a chair with a sign that said "Veteran, Help, Pray." He had his dog on a leash and seemed to be reading the Bible. After his run, Dickie noticed that the man was still there, and he pulled over and stopped. Dickie has a soft spot for veterans, as his father was a World War II Veteran, and at one stage the family was so poor that they were almost homeless. Dickie walked up to the veteran and gave him two twenty-dollar bills and a pair of running shoes. As he passed him the money and shoes, he told him that he had just finished running and the man said he used to run track in high school. He said he can no longer run and pulled up his pant leg to display his prosthesis up to the thigh, and explained he was injured in the Army, but also said he can walk fast. He was trying to apply for disability benefits, but they would not let him in the office with his dog. He said he could not leave the dog outside, because the dog is "the only one who loves me."Dickie told him that he loved him, and the veteran started to cry, and Dickie began to get teary. He told this man to take a good walk with his dog every day because it saves lives and he said he would, and he hugged him and told him he would pray for him.

In the same month, Dickie drove around town and handed out twenty-dollar bills to fifteen homeless people on street corners. Attached to the bill was a note that read,

"This might help you a little, but it will not save your life. I suggest running or walking as much as you can each day to save your life. Running has saved mine at age eighty-two. God Bless you."

Dickie was going to the park to do his weekly three-mile oval run and was getting ready for the 5k race. On his way to the oval, he spotted a young lady sitting on the beach next to her double baby-stroller, where her two infant daughters were sitting. He told her it was good to see her out running with her daughters and she explained that her husband was there to run with her but he just called and said he had to stay late at work. She said they had both not run since they got married five years ago, and they had gained weight and needed to get back to running. She said she couldn't push the old heavy double-stroller someone had given her, and she had been waiting for her husband, who was going to push it for her, but he was running late. Dickie offered to watch the girls or push the stroller so they could run together, and she was grateful. Dickie, who did not realize how heavy the stroller was until he began to push it, felt his arms were going to fall off, but he kept running anyway and they continued to run together on the route. After a few minutes of running, he glanced across and saw that the young mother had tears running down her cheeks—and a big smile, as they were tears of joy, not sadness. After his three-mile run, she hugged and thanked him and told him she was now going to run every day. "Perhaps you could find a stroller that's a little bit lighter," he suggested, and she smiled and nodded in agreement.

On the seventh of January, Dickie went to Sam's Club (a membership warehouse club) and bought five dozen pairs of socks. He then drove through town and gave two pairs of socks, a ten-dollar bill and a note to fifteen homeless people. The note read, "Wear these socks when you go for your run today. God loves you and so do I."

On the twelfth of January 2020, Dickie ran the Extra Yard 5K Race, in which there were 1800 runners registered. This run coincided with the opening of the National Football Championship weekend with a game between LSU and Clemson on Monday in New Orleans. Before the race, he was talking to a couple whose young son was using crutches after spraining his ankle playing seven-on-seven football. After the run, in which the father was involved, Dickie was awarded a standard football with "First Place 2020" printed on it, for his success in the 80+ category. As he was leaving, he saw the boy with the crutches and gave him the football, telling him that he would see him and his dad in a race soon, and wished him good luck at the next football season.

On the 23rd of January, Dickie had just finished going through his speed work at the 400-meter track, (which involved several 200m and 400m runs at a quick pace)when he sat down on the bleachers to watch the track team doing their tryouts. He noticed a young boy sitting near him and they started up a conversation. After chatting for a while, Dickie became aware that the boy was waiting for his brother to finish trying out, as he was not allowed to walk home alone. Both he and his brother lived with their grandmother, and this boy was unable to try out because he did not have any running shoes, due to the cost.

Dickie went to the car and found a pair of shoes and a jacket, as he noticed that the boy's jacket was very thin, and it was cold. Giving them to him, he said, "Try out tomorrow," and he promised he would.

On the January 27, Dickie and his wife Beverley headed out from New Orleans to drive to their condo in Fort Myers, Florida, to be present for their great-grandson's one-month old party. On the way there, they stopped for a restroom break, and on the way to the building noticed a table with military hats and a sign that read, "Donate to the Veterans Relief Fund." Dickie walked up to a man who was standing behind the table and pulled a $20.00 bill out of his money clip. On the day, he was wearing a running shirt that read "Big Easy Running Festival" and on seeing it, the man told Dickie that he used to run everyday up until the previous year. He had stopped because he was too busy with work and the volunteering for the veterans. Dickie gave him twenty dollars, and told him to start running again, encouraging him to run around the parking lot twenty laps. The man had no running shoes, so Dickie ran to the car and brought back a pair of shoes about his size. They fit, and the man thanked Dickie with a smile.

On the February 5, 2020, Dickie was lining up to start a race and began talking to a young couple and their baby son who was in a stroller, who were also in the race. After the race, they came up to Dickie for a chat and told him they only ran one race a year, as the race was to raise money for needy teachers, which they felt was a good cause. Dickie asked them if they would like to run more races, and they said they would, as they really enjoyed it, but could not enter any more races due to the cost. Dickie offered to pay for them to enter a few more races, and they became the first recipients of the Longo Scholarship Fund, a fund Dickie has set up to pay entry fees for deserving runners. The Longo Scholarship Fund gave them a check for one hundred dollars to pay for entry fees for upcoming races, and, not surprisingly, the couple were incredibly happy!

On February 25, Dickie's son and family came to stay with him and Beverley, bringing their grandsons, aged seven, five, and four, to attend the annual Mardi Gras celebration. Dickie was the designated "Uber" driver and dropping them off at the Mardi Gras location, he told them he would be back to pick them up in four hours. Three hours later, he went back an hour early and ran about four miles in the downtown area. He stopped at the parade route to watch for a while, and started talking to a young man, who suddenly ran off to catch up with one of the floats. After he caught up with it, to say hi to a friend of his who was on the float, he returned and Dickie said he must be a runner, the way he ran after the float. The man said he had run in high school. Dickie, noticing his beat-up work shoes, ran back to the car about six blocks away and brought back a pair of running shoes to give the man, and encouraged him to start running again. "I might just do that," he replied with a smile.

On February 27, Dickie's running route took him to the car wash, where he saw the sign holder, who he had previously given shoes and money and told him to run eight blocks. He asked him if he had run, and he replied that he had run ten blocks (about half a mile). Dickie said he was proud of him and he was rewarded with a big smile. Dickie gave him a ten-dollar bill and the man told Dickie he was his best friend. Dickie told him to try and run ten blocks every day, and he sighed, but nodded his head.

Dickie noticed that many runners wrote posts on Facebook about the high price of running race entry fees, and that the fees had put them off running races, or had caused the runners to limit the number of races they run and it upset him. Dickie is so passionate about runners entering races, that he decided to create the Longo Scholarship Fund, which will pay entry fees and purchase running shoes or other help as needed. Since the creation of this fund, Dickie has begun to support many runners with their fees as well as supporting his family and the local community in other areas. This is inspiring kindness around the world.

On March 23, 2020, Dickie returned to his running route. The COVID-19 Pandemic was just beginning to take hold around the world and Dickie was being careful. He knew that there were not many cars on the road and although the car wash was open, he knew his friend would not be making any money. Dickie stopped about six feet away and told him that he was putting two twenty-dollar bills under the stone that was there. He asked about running and the man said he was ready for three miles (perhaps the 5k race that they had talked about). Dickie said in six months, but the man said "now!" Dickie was happy, as it seemed that the man had caught the wonderful running bug.

Dickie saw him again the following day, when he ventured out to get groceries with a white handkerchief around his mouth, and an old pair of fuzzy gloves on his hands, which inspired a few giggles at the store. He drove down to the car wash, where his friend was holding up the car wash sign and stopped on the side of the road. He came over and Dickie put two bags of groceries (Mexican food) on the curb and an envelope with forty dollars in it, and they bowed to each other.

On March 26, Dickie was sitting in his open car garage enjoying the 85-degree temperature and getting ready to go on his hill run later in the day. A young man, of about forty-five years of age, was jogging slowly down his street. Dickie noticed that he was wearing sandals or flip-flops as he ran. Dickie drove down to the end of the block, and passing the runner, he put a pair of training shoes that looked about the right size down next to a stop sign and pointed to them. The man threw his hands up in the air and mouthed "thank you."

After Dickie had posted this on his Facebook page, he received a reply from a man who needed a pair of runners in size twelve. He had been running and walking in work shoes but thought that he probably lived too far away to be eligible for the scholarship fund. Dickie replied and asked him to email his address, and he found out that he lives about 30 miles away. Dickie found him a pair of used running shoes and wrote a note that said "sorry, used shoes, store closed, after virus I will get a new pair for you." Dickie put on his mask and drove to the man's home, placed the shoebox on the front step and ran back to his car. He returned home to an email that read "Thank you, Thank God." The Coronavirus Pandemic was never going to put a stop to Dickie's acts of kindness!

On March 28, 2020, Dickie noticed that the garbage truck was turning the corner into his street, and he ran faster to get home before the truck got there. Running inside, he grabbed three ten-dollar bills, and came back out as the truck arrived. There were three workers, and he gave each of them a ten-dollar bill. Dickie's son is Vice President and lead council for the Waste Management Company, and he knows that they have 83,000 employees worldwide. He is aware of how hard they work and knows how awful it would be if the country shut down garbage collection. After he posted this on Facebook, a few people replied and said they are doing the same and that Dickie has inspired them to be kind.

On March 30, another garbage truck stopped to pick up Dickie's rubbish. Dickie came out to say thank you, and have a quick chat and was told by him that they had to pick up both the garbage can and the large recycling tub, as the council had discontinued the recycling pickup. He told Dickie he worked from 6:00 A.M. to 7:00 P.M. every day and that they were considering going on strike—Dickie is determined to keep tipping them for their work. Then the following day he tipped the mailman and checked to make sure they had a mask and gloves. "I worry about your safety," he told him, "because you are my favorite."

On April 12, 2020, Dickie learned of two people needing help. One, a relative, was fired from his job the day before the COVID-19 Pandemic shutdown, when his owner fired all the employees so he would not have to keep them on the payroll. Filing for unemployment benefits was simply too overwhelming for this man. Dickie sent him a $500 check. The second was a female runner in the Philippines, who needed running shoes to train for an ultra-marathon and could not buy any there due to the store being closed. Dickie ordered a pair online and mailed them to the Philippines. The postage cost half the price of the shoes.

These stories are just examples of many—and throughout 2020, Dickie has continued to find places and moments to spread his kindness, and the Longo Scholarship Fund has been growing in momentum and gathering interest from like-minded people along the way.

One of Dickie's followers, Jason Joubert, gave a description of Dickie as follows.

"Mr. Longo's love for running is infectious. He encourages the youth to get active and love running as a sport, and this opens the doors to health, self-esteem, mental acuity, physical fitness, and the ability to succeed in other sports. He is genuine and honest about his intentions. He is not in it for notoriety or pats on the back, but he does what he does to better our world. How couldn't he inspire others?"[1] These are words that reflect those of many of Dickie's family, friends, and followers, and I'm sure that there would be untold numbers of people whom Dickie has influenced over his life, in the avenues of work, sport, and family (each of which have at many times overlapped.)

Dickie began a Facebook page a few years ago, as a way of motivating others and he has since developed a huge following, with well over four thousand friends, and each post he makes attracts comments from his friends and followers who find inspiration in what he shares. For example, Dickie will

---

[1] Jason Joubert, 11/03/20, email to author.

share details of his races, and then the stats (such as in 2018, when he wrote: "At eighty years old I run a race every weekend. Ran fifty-one last year and won fifty in my age division of seventy-four to seventy-nine and eighty plus. If I can do it, so can every one of you."

As many runners know, and many people know in general, it is easy to find excuses to not run, and not remain active. Dickie is remarkable in the way he has maintained an ongoing ability to fight that inner voice, that can convince us in all sorts of ways not to do what we need to do, and still get out the door, in all kinds of weather. Someone asked him how he could run five miles at 4:00 P.M. every day in the heat and bright sun of New Orleans. His answer to that was "at eighty-two, this old Italian skin is like leather now and the sun can't penetrate," and finished with "as Nike says, 'Just do it.'"

In 1971, Dickie took a job at a large Catholic school as a Public Relations and Fundraising Director. Most of the fundraising came from the alumni (graduates or former students of the school) and Dickie decided he wanted to get the current students involved as well. To kick it off, he put out an announcement that he was going to run laps around the quad at lunchtime, and all of the students were to come out and throw money inside the quad area, for each lap that he ran. Most students thought he would run ten to fifteen laps, but instead he ran for an hour (about six miles) and raised about five hundred dollars. In a recent race, a runner came up to Dickie and said he threw coins at him at the school back then and that watching him run that day had inspired him to run and tryout for the track team, and that his buddy had also tried out, and that ever since, he had been running! When asked by one of his followers on Facebook if any of the coins thrown had hit him, Dickie replied that they had but most did not because he was so fast. He did get hit with a silver dollar, which he kept to himself, saying "to the victors go the spoils—the joys of running!"

Dickie's friend Allan Robertson is one of those who has been inspired by Dickie Longo. Allan is fifty-eight years of age, and has run for his entire life, but always kept to himself. He would simply run the race, get his time, and go home and never took up the opportunity to talk to other runners. The only interest he had was to beat his previous times for that distance and if he were not in his top form and ready to set a personal record (PR), he would not run the race. This went on for many years, until several years ago when he had a terrible running injury where he pulled a hamstring, and it put him out of action for many years. During this time off running, Allan gained about 100lbs (45kgs). Eventually he began walking again and slowly got back to running, but this was awfully slow progress.

Returning to the races, Allan was keeping to himself. He had always noticed the "cheery old well-dressed guy," who always had a matching outfit and perfect hair before or after the race. He had admired how he would see Dickie at all the races, from Thibodaux, Assumption, All New Orleans, north Shore to South Shore—Dickie was at every race. He always noticed how differently he ran from the way he himself did—he was evidently running because he enjoyed himself. Everywhere he went, everybody knew him, and he was loved by all. At every race, Allan got closer and closer to catching the "dapper fellow," but he was tough. One day, Allan finally beat him to the finish, and Dickie came up to him and said he'd been watching him for a while, and saw how he had been losing weight and getting faster, and how proud he was of him. Allan was floored, amazed that this man had taken time out to give him encouragement. Dickie said he should meet some of Dickie's friends for continued support and introduced him to some runners.

It was this way that Dickie explained how important the running community is, describing it as a family—the bigger the better. Each race after this, Allan would arrive earlier and stay later, and now he has joined multiple running clubs and organizations. He has made hundreds of running friends and has never been so motivated in his life. Allan will go to races whether he is in top form or has missed several days of training and he credits Dickie with having taught him to see the big picture, to stop being so concerned about himself and to focus on encouraging others. Allan now considers Dickie to be one of his dearest friends, and always reserves time to go and chat with him at every race.

Dickie always notices when people display the same courtesy to him that he displays to others. For example, recently he was running around a couple of blocks and noticed a couple sitting in lawn chairs in the driveway, sitting out in the sun. The older guy said,

"I see you run by here all the time. How old are you?" Dickie answered he was soon to be 84. The man said, "Eighty-four, and caught in a forty-three-year-old body!" Dickie felt stunned, and then ran a little faster than normal.

"Maybe a little compliment here and there lifts the spirit a little, let's try it when safe to do so.'"

"Thanks to Dickie," Allan wrote, "I run for all the right reasons now and can go to a race anywhere and be surrounded by friends. Dickie Longo is a great ambassador to the sport, and I will be forever in his debt."

Another runner who has been inspired by Dickie, is Liz Schilleci. Liz lives in Kenner, Louisiana, and has been a runner for about thirty years. She met Dickie at one of the New Orleans races on a bus ride home from the finish line. They spent some time getting to know each other and she immediately liked him and could tell that he was an incredibly special person. Liz said she saw Dickie at many of the New Orleans races and would make it a point to say hello. Liz has been following Dickie on Facebook and has come to understand his passion for running and his desire to help save lives "one at a time." She is aware that Dickie believes that God puts him in places to serve others and she honestly believes this. Liz admires his efforts of being an active runner and trying to make a difference in people's lives through his passion and she feels inspired to emulate this as she gets older.

"Dickie is an inspiration to many in the running community and beyond," Liz wrote. "I'm glad God put him in my path so that I could learn to be a better person."

Charli Guest is another runner, who believes that Dickie makes God's love visible by his actions every day, and she has stayed to watch him get his awards despite him saying that by the time his age group would be called everyone would have gone home.

On April 12, 2020, Dickie set out for a run on a newly constructed route, a six-foot-wide concrete path in the medium lane of a four-lane boulevard, which is about two miles in length. After running a mile, he saw a young lady runner coming towards him and when she got about six feet from him, she stopped and told him that she had seen him running in the neighborhood, and that she has seen him on Facebook and that he is a legend.

They discussed whether they would run a virtual race and then Dickie agreed to do a virtual 5k with her. They ran with the young lady about ten feet ahead of him, and Dickie ran in at 32:14 for the 5km, which he wasn't ashamed of. She called out 'thanks for the motivation!" Dickie blew her a kiss and reflected that a good way to run a virtual race was to "get a pacer who is fifty-five years younger than you!"

On May 18, 2020, Dickie decided to go the only park that was open to run, at 5:30 P.M. the park has a nice two-mile oval running along the edge of the park, which Dickie would usually run twice to get in his four miles. The entrance to the park is right across the highway from the car wash where his "card-holding friend" sits. Dickie parked in the lot and walked up to the track. There sitting on a bench was the card holder. Dickie stood back about 8 ft. (due to the ongoing COVID-19 Pandemic social distancing safety needs) and asked him why he was there. He said he ran one time around and now he was going to run home. It is about a mile home for him. Noticing that he was wearing the older pair of running shoes Dickie had given him about eight months ago, he told him to stay there, and went to his car to pick up a better pair of shoes, a twenty-dollar bill and a singlet shirt. The weather was about ninety degrees and Dickie knew that his friend needed a cooler shirt to run in. He ran back to him and placed the stuff on end of bench, then invited him to pick it up. His friend said what he did when he had first helped him, "You great man."

Dickie could be considered a true leader, demonstrating through his everyday actions and in the stories he shares. He has a strong character and an inner strength, combined with strong moral values, and his life exemplifies one of a true leader, who is celebrated not by the mind, but of the "tone of the heart."[2]

One example of this was in an incident in September 2019. Dickie was out on his daily five-mile run, moving along a little used road on the right side. He noticed two bikers riding towards him on the other side of the road, in "fancy bikers' outfits." Dicky was struggling as he ran up the hill, while the bikers were on the way down, when suddenly, they crossed the road and were heading in Dickie's direction, as if to collide with him. Determined to remain calm and unaffected, Dickie decided to stand his ground and keep running, refusing to move from the side of the road. When they got within a few feet of him, when a man of less inner strength would have run away, they suddenly swerved and laughed, and Dickie, cheekily called out "Wimps!" Thecyclists swerved back around and rode up to him.

"What did you call us?" one of them said in a threatening tone.

Dickie replied, "Until you can run five miles in 98 degrees uphill, you are not working hard. Cycling is fifty percent coasting." They rode off, unsure how to react to this man who continued to run, unaffected by their attempt to frighten him.

---

[2] Max DePree 'Leadership is an Art' 2004, Currency Publications.

In March 2020, the COVID-19 pandemic began to change Dickie's life, as it was changing the lives (and unfortunately, taking the lives) of many people around the world. Dickie has maintained his inner strength throughout this challenging time. In March, he wrote on Facebook that the governor had put out a decree that everyone must stay in the house, and only go out for essential reasons such as buying groceries or medications. Dickie said he was going to add a third essential reason—to run his daily four miles. He believes that if everyone would run every day, they would not need so many medications and they would also need less groceries, and he credits his own sixty-year running journey to his excellent health, no medications and his weight of 139 pounds (63kgs) at the age of eighty-three. "Let us run the virus out of town!" was his own decree.

Dickie once wrote, "Why are runners such a great group?"

His answer? "Because they respect each other so much," and this can be seen in how they converse and referred to some phrases he often hears amongst his running friends—"I am proud of you." "What is your opinion?""If you please.""Thank you'" and the rare use of the word *I*.

Dickie says that he approaches every race likes he approaches life in general, through his faith, training, tenacity, and encouragement. For faith, he says, "we cannot see the finish line until the end, but we must believe it is there—so it is in life." For training, he says "'If done right, our race will result in a good finish, just as in the life we live, if done right, will also result in a good finish."

Tenacity—his quote, "In a race, keep going when everything in you says quit, and this is the same in life, especially when you are faced with huge obstacles" (such as the COVID-19 pandemic).

In encouragement: "If we give encouragement to other runners in a race, we will all be champions—and this is the same in life."

On May 27,2020—(Dickie's 83rd Birthday), he received many birthday greetings on his Facebook page. Two of them stood out, as they reflect the influence that Dickie has had on people across the world.

Farrah Boudreaux wrote: "Happy birthday to one of the sweetest, most supportive people that I've ever met, and whose backstory is just incredible. I love hearing your stories!"

Roy Aubin wrote: "You are spot-on (referring to the previous comment). Short story, couple of years ago at a River Shack Run on East bank, me and Carson had finished and were waiting for Toshia. Dickie Longo started a casual conversation with Carson about nothing and everything. He was dreading the walk down the levee to the River shack, but Carson, being equally sweet, said she would help, and they walked arm in arm down the level. He kept chatting with us the rest of the evening. Carson Aubin was like, 'he is so nice!' I hope we are all like that at (83)."

And indeed—if we all turned out like Dickie Longo, what a great place this world would be to live in, for runners and non-runners alike!

Running Story One – Adam Fulton

I started running about ten years ago after I quit smoking.I started doing 5ks, 10ks and even half marathons, not to mention Warrior Dash and Tough Mudder, of which I did several. After my second divorce, I started to let myself go, and eventually stopped running for four years, subsequentlybecoming the heaviest I've been in my life, with the scales going from one hundred and ninety pounds to two hundred and eighty-five pounds. Things were not looking too good health wise, in fact, in January I was diagnosed with diabetes, I weighed the most I haveever weighed, and I knew something had to change. I decided, right after receiving the diagnosis, to start running again, as a part of my plan to improve my health and lose weight.

I had to start from scratch.I started walking in my neighbourhood for half an hour at a time, going from one mile, to two miles, then three. I went from a walk, to a brisk walk to a walk-run and eventually built to full-blown running (or jogging). My times started to improve and my distances got longer.I worked up to running my first three miles without breaking, then improved to four, then five miles each run. During this time, I also started hiking and regularly going to the gym, and all was going great until COVID-19 struck.

The gyms closed, and even worse, I contracted the disease myself. I was sick for two weeks, and it took another two weeks to recover enough to run again. My doctor advised I don't run for the month after just to be safe, so I felt like I'd gone backwards in my progress, which was incredibly frustrating! So, when I finally got back out there, I had to almost start from scratch. With the right mindset, though, my progress was quick, and now I'm running longer and faster than I have ever run. I look forward to each run, challenging myself to see what improvements I can gain and accomplish.

I chose to run, rather than weightlifting or CrossFit, because I like the challenges it brings me to strengthen my body and mind.I love running outdoors, in the mornings.It's the perfect way to start my day, get my thoughts together, to have time to think—essentially, I use it as a form a meditation.I find, I am most at peace with myself as I can be alone with my thoughts while pushing myself daily.When I run, in my neighbourhood, I set a minimum number of miles I want to accomplish, and then I just hit the road and crush it. Some days I do the miles I set and most days I keep running, exceeding my goals. Being outside, running, is the best form of therapy I have found.

When I posted on Facebook about my accomplishments, Dickie responded and was really encouraging, and I really appreciate him doing this. I am extremely proud of how far I have come and if my story and drive can inspire or push someone to achieve their goals, I'm all about it and am always more than willing to help.

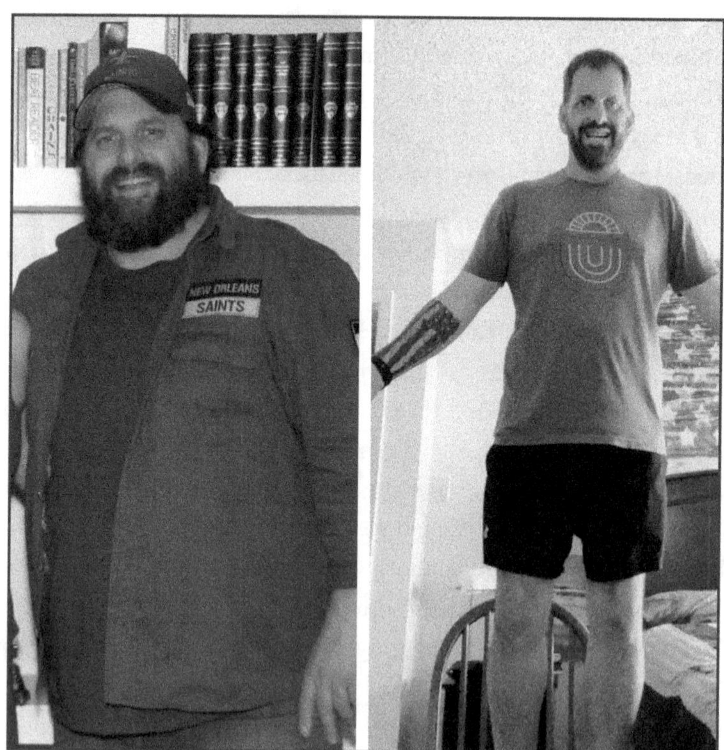

Adam Fulton 'Before and After'

CHAPTER TWO

Early childhood
and relationship with his father

Thirteen years after his mother walked out on his father, his brother, and himself, Dickie saw her at his wedding. It would be the second-to-last time she saw him in his life.

Glancing at her from across the church, he saw an "older, grey-haired lady" enter the building, and didn't think much of it until his brother Bob said, "I think that might be Mom."

Dickie did not recognize her, and by the time the wedding reception had begun, after marrying the love of his life, he realized she had again disappeared from his life and he didn't see her again until she came to visit in New Orleans, many years later, stating that she wanted to tell Dickie and his brother Bob why she abandoned them. Dickie waited in anticipation for an explanation, excuse, or reason, that might make it all make sense. But instead, he was left unsatisfied as she went home without any explanation, later blaming him for a health complaint she had developed since the visit. At her funeral in New York, after she died at the age of ninety-five, Dickie met his halfbrother and halfsister for the first time.

Growing up without a mother was no doubt something that shaped Dickie's early life and indeed, Dickie's childhood experience was not a traditional one, in any sense.

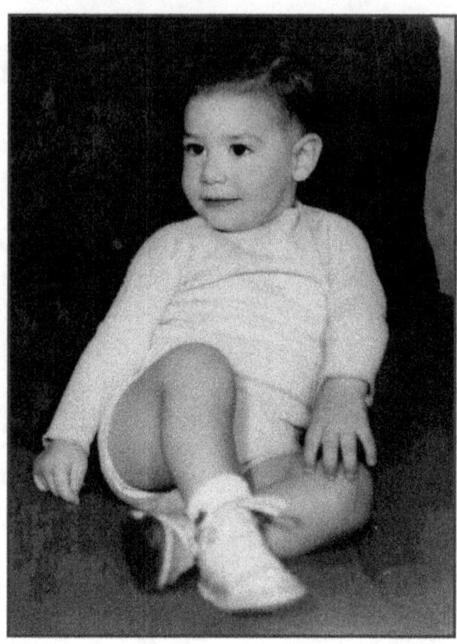

Dickie Longo, 1938, aged approx. 18 months, studio photograph.

He was born in Cedar Rapids, Iowa, in 1937, and named Gary Richard (Dickie) Longo, the first of two sons to Henry Albert Longo and Betty Belnap. Henry had lived in three towns before moving to Iowa, an agricultural, corn-growing town in the Midwestern United States, bordered by the Mississippi River, to the east and the Missouri River and Big Sioux River to the west. [3] Iowa, before white settlement (with first "discovery" in 1673 and full white settlement in mid-1800s) had long been home to many Native Americans, with approximately seventeen different Indian tribes in residence. These tribes include the Ioway, Sauk, Mesquaki, Sioux, Potawatomi, Oto, and Missouri. [4] The town developed as an agricultural region, with a diversified production and is largely known for its successful production of corn. [5]

In 1938, when their eldest son was around one year old, Henry and Betty Longo packed up house and travelled to Southeast Florida in two cars with trailers, bringing along their parents (Dickie's grandparents), three uncles, and

---

[3] Wikipedia, accessed 05-04-20, https://en.wikipedia.org/wiki/Iowa#Depression,_World_War_II_and_manufacturing,_1930%E2%80%931985

[4] Schweider, Dorothy 'History of Iowa,' in 'Iowa Official Registry,' accessed 05-04-20, http://publications.iowa.gov/135/1/history/7-1.html

[5] Schweider, Dorothy (see footnote 3)

an aunt. Dickie's father longed to open a fresh orange juice business, and Florida, with a climate ideal for growing juicy oranges—with "subtropical temperatures, abundant sunshine, distinctive sandy soil, and ample rainfall,"[6] seemed the perfect place for such an endeavor. (The Florida citrus industry currently contributes $8.6 million to the state of Florida and supports 45,000 jobs).

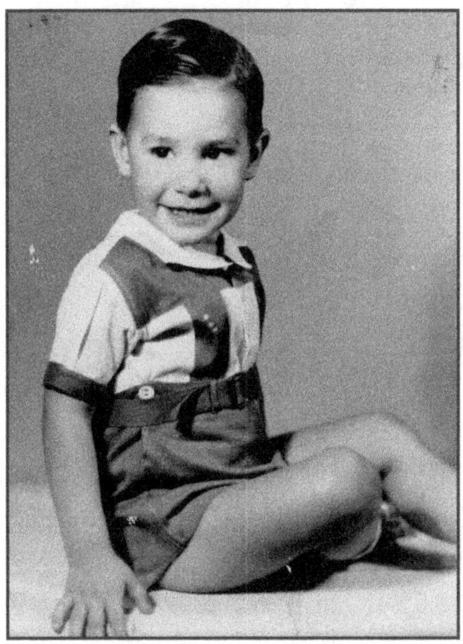

Dickie Longo, 1940, studio photograph

Things were looking rosy, or should we say "zesty," for the Longo family, however unfortunately the political climate was not conducive to such success, and the onset of the Second World War was an unexpected turn of events. Dickie's father, Henry, knowing he was going to be drafted, joined the Navy, preferring this option to the less secure one of being drafted into the Army, where he was likely to have been sent to the foreign frontline of battle. This turned out to be a timely move, as he was stationed at the Great Lakes Naval post as an aeronautics engineer, where his job was to repair airplanes. He spoke fondly of his military experience, though it eventually cost him his marriage.

---

[6] Florida Citrus, Florida Department of Citrus, 2018, https://www.floridacitrus.org /newsroom/citrus-411/weather/benefits-of-the-florida-climate/ viewed 21-03-20

Dickie remembers his mother being upset because she had to work as a waitress while his father was in service, to keep the family afloat financially, a job which she found unsatisfying and about which she often complained. Dickie remembers returning from school and the playground (where he and his brother would go to do their afternoon fitness activities), to find that she had already gone to work, leaving them both to fend for themselves until the morning, when she would return from her shift work.

During this time, she met naval officer to whom she rented a spare room in the house, while he was stationed at Fort Lauderdale in Florida, and they fell in love. When Henry returned from war, Betty had a suitcase ready in the hallway and left as soon as he arrived, later filing for divorce.

After their mother left, Dickie recalls that his father, Henry, never dated and did not remarry, as he was focused on raising his sons. This decision perhaps reflected his beliefs that marriage should be for life, as Henry, with his Italian background, was quite strong in his religious beliefs. Dickie and his brother Bob were sent to Trinity Lutheran School in Fort Lauderdale, Florida, for elementary school, a school for disadvantaged children. The school consisted of one room, with fourth-, fifth-, and sixth-grade students in one room. The fourth-grade students sat in rows one and two, fifth in three and four, and sixth in rows five and six. He sat at a standard desk with an inkwell and pencil slot, and his teacher was Ms. Waterman.

Each row of students would listen to the other row's lessons, and Dickie took the opportunity to take in as much of the other classes as he could. This was quite a lonely period for Dickie and his brother, Bob, and he had few friends, but later he moved to the Southside Elementary School and Fort Lauderdale High School, where he found his feet, and with his athletic prowess, he quickly grew in popularity, and things began to look up for both him and Bob. Dickie was voted "Most Athletic" in his senior year, at a large school of 2000 students, which was no small achievement.

One funny story that Dickie relates was in high school, when he injured his thumb playing football. He was sporting a bandage on his thumb, which was the perfect excuse to be sent to the library during typing class, where he would just hang out and then leave as soon as the bell rang, allowing him to be first in the lunchline, quite a privilege at the time. Eventually, of course, his thumb healed, but being somewhat on the cheeky side, Dickie would put the bandage back on, and the teacher continued to send him to the library, a trick he got away with for an entire semester! In the meantime, he was out on the football field, passing footballs without any problem—apparently the typing teacher was not one for watching the sporting games.

With his father away, Dickie was increasingly relied upon to care for his younger brother, Bob. When Dickie's father returned home from his Naval Service after WWII ended, Dickie recalls that he and Bob were thrilled. He believes that his father had sent them letters during his time away, but unfortunately Betty had failed to pass them on to them or answer them.It was just before Christmas, and with no money for gifts, Dickie's father announced, sadly, "There will be no Christmas this year, we can't even afford a Christmas tree."But Dickie and Bob didn't mind, because their dad was home, and to them, that was the real Christmas gift in any case.

On Christmas morning, Dick and Bob were usually expected to go out and bring in the paper, a job for which they had long established a routine of taking turns. But this time, their father asked them to both go out together. This, of course, piqued their curiosity as it was such a stark break in their usual routine, nevertheless, out they went, through the front door to the porch. It only took a second before they looked to the right and saw two brand-new Schwinn bikes, one red and one green.

Dickie could not stop the tears that began to flow, as to him this was not just a bike, but a whole new opportunity. He could now ride to school instead of walking, take on a morning paper route to help bring in money for his family, and best of all, ride to the playground where he could do a five-mile run. The bikes were the icing on the cake of having their father home from the war, and a salve to ease the sadness that had entered the house when their mother left, for good.

Dickie's only source of money as a child and teenagercame from his paper route, which he shared with his brother Bob. Dickie's father was saving up to open a small used-car lot and he made it clear that Dickie was expected to work on the cars lot he would show up every Saturday morning, after a hard ball game, to help, because that was expected—and unpaid.

Dickie described his father's discipline style as "old school." There was a tree in their backyard that was a source of "whips"—the branches were mostly sticks. Dickie's father would break off a stick and whip him and his brother, Bob, when they were disobedient, leaving the tree quite bare. In those days, "softer" forms of discipline and behavior management were not as common, as Dickie describes it, "there was no such thing as time-out." Dickie believes that the style of discipline that they experienced, though harsh, has carried over into his running career, and believes that a runner must "exhibit great discipline to be successful." Dickie has certainly achieved a lot, so this mantra has proven to be successful for him, although in no way would he want to promote the use of corporal punishment in parenting and encourages parents today to find more loving and appropriate ways to provide boundaries for their children.

Dickie may have inherited some genetic advantages from his father, as, like his son, he had been a terrific runner in high school.He had been on a pathway to run in college, but unfortunately an injury held him back. He later became an avid walker, often walking for hours at a time. At the age of eighty-eight, he was still walking, and with a slight case of dementia, made quite a scene one day when he could not find his way home.

Luckily, a policeman to whom he was familiar, saw him sitting on the street corner crying and took him home. After this, he could not go on walks by himself anymore, and Dickie recalled that it "broke his heart." One morning, he went outside to collect the morning paper, and slipped on a wet stepping-stone, falling, and breaking his hip. At hospital, he had his hip reset, but contracted pneumonia from another patient, sadly succumbing to it within a week.

Dickie now dedicates every race to his "wonderful Dad" and prefers to remember the positive moments he spent with him than any of the harsher moments. For some of us, it is easier to recall the more challenging memories of our childhood and youth, memories that evoke emotions such as sadness or anger. But Dickie finds it difficult to do this. When encouraged to recall some more difficult memories about his father, Dickie somewhat reluctantly explained that things became very tense between him and his father, and that after he had gone to college without his father's blessings, he rarely returned home.

His brother, Bob, on the other hand, stayed on with his father, working in the used-car business, which went on to become remarkably successful. Dickie recalled somewhat wistfully, "my father became a millionaire, and my brother went on to do very nicely out of this." Evidently, there is sadness, and angst, in amidst the lovely memories Dickie has of his dad. But he chooses not to dwell, on them, instead being grateful for all the blessings he has received.

Dickie's own experience of being a dad, is one that he treasures. Dickie has three sons, Reed (58), Rob (55), and Ross (44). He also has a number of grandchildren, Ryan (30), Mia (27), Callie (22), Ella (19), Kiki (18), Matthew (7), Charlie (5), and William (4), and one great-grandchild, (all ages at time of writing – April 2020), Luca, aged one.

A story he has told, which illustrates Dickie's lovely commitment to and connection with his sons, is when his second son, Rob, was about five. They had a routine of reading a bedtime story, and then saying prayers together. After the prayer, he would tell Rob that he loved him very much. He would say "I love you one hundred times,"Rob would say "I love you a million,"Dickie would say "I love you a billion,"Rob would say "I love you a trillion." Then Rob would be quiet for a while, before he replied,"Daddy, I love you until there are no more numbers."

Dickie is a father, a grandfather and (at the time of writing), soon to be great-grandfather. His wife Beverley was invited to the baby shower, and she bought a gift for the baby. Dickie bought a different gift—a pair of running shoes size 0-3 months, and in the box, he put a note, "please find baby Luca's first pair of running shoes and a race medal. Please hang it in his room and place this note in his baby book. When Luca is nine years old, I will be ninety years old, and we will run a 5k race together and call it the ninety and nine race. Show this note to him each year, so he will run and train and get ready for our race together nine years from now." This is an example of how Dickie's spirit will carry on through future generations when he is gone. For it is his positive attitude and vision for each person, to be the best they can be, which inspires so many. What a lucky baby young Luca is, to have such a great, great-grandfather to inspire him!

It may sound to some as though Dickie is a little running obsessed, and certainly, running is a huge focus for him in his life. But he is a family man, first and foremost, and is often guided by the wisdom and advice of his wife. For example, in the Christmas of 2019, he and Beverley travelled to Dallas, Texas, to spend time with their son and family, including three grandsons aged seven, five, and three. It is a family tradition for them to go to the Christmas Eve Church service at the Highland Park United Methodist Church. Dickie had planned to run a race that morning and then go to the evening service but was instead informed by his son that they were going to a special children's service at 10:15 A.M. Despite the disappointment that he was likely to have felt, Dickie cancelled his race entry.

"There will be many races to run," he wrote on his Facebook page. "I don't know how many more chances I will have to go to a Christmas Eve Service with my beautiful family, God only knows," and he then proceeded to wish his running friends and followers a merry Christmas, and send his blessings.

Dickie credits his hard-working attitude to something his dad had told him about seventy years ago. He said, "If you want to be good at something, you have to work hard at it."

"He meant to *really* work hard at it! I am trying to outwork every eighty-three-year-old runner anywhere! I'm glad I listened to my dad; he was a great man."

Running Story two – Judith Powell

I have a story for you. Not too long ago, I was looking at a track at a nearby Middle School, thinking, "Someday I would love to be able to run from my house to the track (about a mile), and then around the track at least once."

Guess what—two weekends ago, I did it! I ran and ran! I did the virtual Long Island Half Marathon and I finished, with a "not bad" time for a sixty-year-old woman who started running at the age of sixty.

Every time I wanted to stop, I kept thinking "I can't disappoint Dickie!" So I pushed myself.

Thanks Buddy. [7]

---

[7] From a post on Dickie's Facebook page by Judith, shared with writer on 7th October 2020.

For the love of sport

Dickie Longo, 1955, Fort Lauredale HS, Voted 'Most Athletic'.

Dickie's physical presence at races every weekend of the year has become a motivational factor for many. During the lockdowns in the COVID-19 pandemic of 2020, Dickie had to withdraw to his home for safety, and many of the races that he loves were cancelled. But this did not stop him from continuing to inspire and motivate, and he continued to use Facebook to communicate a sense of hope to his running community.

Dickie is all-in and all-out a sportsman, and a tough one at that, often withstanding painful injuries and getting back up on the field regardless, something we see in his running—that sense of drive, that determination to keep training and racing through all kinds of weather and all kinds of world events. Nothing is going to stop him!

Dickie was a freshman at high school in 1951 and was holding the position of third-string quarterback on the football team. Sitting on the bench, he was called in by his coach to join in the game, after first- and second-string got hurt. He was so scared that when he got up off the bench there was a wet spot—he had indeed wet his pants! But he went out there regardless and ran as fast as possible to save his life, and from then on was placed in the position of starting quarterback.

Another time, in senior year, Dickie was throwing a pass and was hit in his arm, dislocating his shoulder. He went to the bench, where his coach strapped his arm across his chest. He was sent straight back out as running back, when the running back had an injury, and his coach instructed him to fall onto his left side when tackled. To save his head, he had to run fast—and he puts his running speed down to saving his life! Luckily, the team won the game and he ended up making All Conference.

Many athletes who show drive and resilience at the level Dickie has, and continues to show today as a runner, have had some sort of hardship in their early lives that has helped them to become stronger and more resilient. Dickie is no exception. He began early, by running to deliver papers. By the age of ten, he had begun to play Little League baseball, football, and basketball, in addition to running in the playground track team. He continued in these sports into high school, lettering in all four of them for three years. (For those that aren't familiar, to letter in a sport means that you have received an award for your achievement and dedication in a sport, in the form of an initial made from cloth, usually the first letter of the name of a school or university, which is to be sewn onto the recipient's coat or sweater). [8] In college, Dickie played basketball and baseball on full scholarship, entitling him to free college tuition. He now holds a master's degree in Physical Education.

Sometimes Dickie used his athletic prowess to help him move ahead in unexpected ways. One time in his English class, in 1956, his professor said she had seen him running around campus. She lived across the street from him and she offered to tutor him and share a hot chocolate. She had been a runner herself, but at sixty-eight years of age, now preferred to walk. This partnership helped him advance in a subject that he had found challenging.

---

[8] Grammarphobia, accessed 05-04-20, https://www.grammarphobia.com/blog/2012/08/lettering-in-sports.html

Another opportunity came when, in his sophomore year, Dickie was taking European History and was captain of the college baseball team. One day his history professor asked him to come to his office after class. Dickie was worried, thinking he was going to be in trouble for his lack of academic prowess. But the meeting led to a discussion about baseball, as it turned out that the professor had played baseball at Harvard and was simply keen to talk about his experience and had noted how well Dickie was doing on the team. This built their relationship and Dickie ended up with an A in that class, going on to take a history minor. He has often found that his sporting prowess was a great way to meet people, connect, and sometimes give him that upward push.

Not content with having mastered these sports, after college, Dickie taught himself to play tennis, and went on to enjoy this sport for forty years, winning over three hundred tournaments. His routine was to play singles for about two hours, followed by a three-mile run. He later took up doubles, when his son, Reed, entered them in the national Father-Son doubles championships, and they won district tournament and regional tournament, and were also invited to play in national tournament at the US Open tournament in New York in 1980. There they met John McEnroe, Björn Borg, and other great players, and placed well, achieving a national ranking.

Dickie's goal, when he began to play tennis, was to win many tournaments. In 2017, when interviewed for the *Picayune Times*, Dickie had won280 tennis tournaments, and was rated number two in the state and number eight in the South by the United States Tennis Association in his age group. [9] He began at the age of forty-five, stating, "I wanted a sport that would give me an opportunity to compete and one where I could get plenty of exercise. I thought about golf, but it didn't seem like I would get much exercise on the golf course."

He went on to win the state Senior Olympics tennis championships in his age group for twenty consecutive years. The tennis director at the Metairie Beach Club, Ski Chelchowski, stated, "Dick is a fantastic tennis player, and he's in great shape. He wears his opponents down with his fitness and his power of concentration."[10]

Dickie looks back at his childhood as one that, whilst involving many challenges, also offered many opportunities. At the age of ten, for example, Dickie

---

[9] Hodges, Earl, The Times, Picayune, 16/07/2017.
[10] See citation 9, above.

was running on the playground track team. Playgrounds in the USA were established with the use of public funding and the playground movement emphasized the relationship between organized play, health, character, and democracy, particularly in poor, urban areas. They were based on a theory that "building character on the playground benefited society as well as the individual."[11] It is likely that Dickie has turned out to be a prime example of the type of person that the founders of this movement wanted to nurture.

Dickie benefited from having an established supervised playground in his local area, which stood him in good stead for building his athletic prowess. The history of this playground is fascinating. In New Orleans, Louisiana, during World War II, a group of civic-minded men banded together to give the city a planned recreation program. Schoolgrounds, which were normally closed for vacation periods, were opened as supervised playgrounds, and vacant lots were converted into neighborhood play spots, with civic groups providing equipment.

In 1947, a city ordinance was passed setting up the official New Orleans Recreation Department with Lester Lautenschlager, a former Tulane University Football Star, as its director. These playgrounds quickly increased from thirty-three to ninety-one in number and included large gymnasiums, floodlighting systems, swimming pools, recreation centers, field houses, baseball fields, and football fields, as well as play-spots with swings, merry-go-rounds, jumble towers, and sand pits.

They provided a wide range of sports and also other activities, including arts and crafts, music, dramatics, and dancing, as well as more traditional athletics and activities to suit all ages. [12] Without this playground providing him with opportunities, would Dickie have had the opportunity to develop his athletic skills? Perhaps not.

As a runner, Dickie has shown ongoing dedication. As a ten-year-old, he had no running shoes, as his family could not afford to buy shoes just for

---

[11] Anderson, Linnea M. (2006). "'The playground of today is the republic of tomorrow": Social reform and organized recreation in the USA, 1890-1930s' *The encyclopedia of pedagogy and informal education*, https://infed.org/mobi/social-reform-and-organized-recreation-in-the-usa/.

[12] Wilson, Kenneth, in *The Rotarian*, June 1950, accessed online 05-04-20, https://books.google.com.au/books?id=C0YEAAAAMBAJ&pg=PA29&lpg=PA29&dq=new+orleans+supervised+playground&source=bl&ots=KKESlC4P0m&sig=ACfU3U0LsSGQ9TC3EcF6R1iesDNBDjezng&hl=en&sa=X&ved=2ahUKEwj7pbDS-9DoAhVEIbcAHf5uDF8Q6AEwAnoECAwQKQ#v=onepage&q=new%20orleans%20supervised%20playground&f=false

running. He and his brother each had a pair of old Chuck Taylor Converse tennis shoes, one day his track coach found an old pair of running shoes in the locker room that someone had thrown away and gave them to Dickie. The same happened for his baseball spikes. He is proud to now own four pairs of running shoes, but never forgets those early days of scarcity.

Dickie credits his wife, Beverley, as his initial motivating force to start running, stating, "I was a newlywed, and looked at my wife, and she was in such great shape and looked so good, I asked myself what I could do to keep up with her." Not wanting to get "fat and sloppy," he started running the very next day! [13]Dickie began to race around twenty-eight years ago, and in the last few years, has averaged forty-five races per year, where he mainly concentrates on the distance of 5k. One of his joys is the camaraderie of other runners, many of them years younger than himself. Dickie himself has stated that "runners are some of the greatest people I've ever met," and he often speaks of the way runners motivate and encourage each other. He describes many of the people he has met at races as his best friends and credits them for encouraging him to keep improving.

Dickie's running adventures have spanned the globe, and he has run in countries including England, France, Italy, Switzerland, Ireland, Scotland, Netherlands, Germany, and Australia. His family of origin emigrated to America in 1906 from Palermo, Sicily, and he had long wanted to go back to the old country to see where the family had come from. This opportunity came when he and Beverley travelled to Europe and included Rome in one of their stops, where they stayed in a hotel a few blocks from the Tiber River.

One afternoon on this holiday, Dickie began his afternoon five-mile run and found a nice running path along the river. On the way to the path, he picked out landmarks at each street turn, because there were no street signs. At one turn there was a bike shop, which he felt he would easily recall on his way back. On his return, however, he noticed that all the stores were closed, and their windows shuttered, and he discovered that they close every day from 12:00 P.M. to 3:00 P.M. for the nap and rest time. He missed some turns, and the bike shop was nowhere to be seen, and he soon lost his bearings. Luckily, a nice man helped him find his way back to the hotel, and Dickie was surprised to find that he did not wait for his tip.

---

[13] Hodges, Earl, in *The Times – Picayune*, 16/07/2017.

In 2005, Dickie was attending an Ulster Project Conference in Northern Ireland. The Ulster project was started in 1975 by Reverend Stephen Kent Jacobson of the Episcopal Church in the US and the Reverend Kerry Waterstone, a Church of Ireland priest, in Tullamore, County Offaly, Republic of Ireland. The purpose of the project was to develop harmony between the rival religious groups of Anglicans and Catholics, and provide a safe place in the United States of America for Teenagers from Northern Ireland to discuss the climate of "The Troubles" that were facing them at home.

It had original success in Connecticut then spread to other member cities across the United States.[14] This project continues to run today, offering leadership training in conflict resolution, with the goal of empowering Ulster Project teens to work against discrimination in all of its forms. This movement has grown from the original guidelines which were directed against the Catholic and Protestant conflicts in Northern Ireland, and now aims to promote tolerance and respect across all of the "lines that divide us," with a goal to create "unity amidst diversity."[15] Dickie advised that twenty-four students would attend the project each year, and each day would attend various planned events, many with a purpose of working together on some sort of project—a tangible way of placing Protestants and Catholics side by side to show the world that they can live in harmony.

In 2005, the host families (families would act as hosts for two years, when the students would come to New Orleans for a month), were invited to attend the first Ulster Project Conference in Londonderry. This was a kind of reunion for the families who had hosted students since the year 2000, when the project had first taken foot in New Orleans. Dickie and Beverley travelled to Londonderry and stayed with the family of the student they had hosted. Dickie described it as a "great trip and a wonderful experience."

During a break in the conference, Dickie decided to go for a run in the city (the second largest city in Northern Ireland), to the place where there is a wall separating the Catholics and the Protestants. This famous and historical wall is about fifteen feet wide with plenty of room to run and walk on. He set off on his run and after completing one lap he was about to start a second (aiming for four laps of around four miles), when he noticed a row of teens who had just been dismissed from high school had begun to form a barrier, locked

---

[14] Wikipedia, viewed 19-04-20 https://en.wikipedia.org/wiki/Ulster_Project
[15] Ulster Project International, viewed 19-04-20, http://www.ulsterproject.org/

arm in arm, across the fifteen-foot-wide structure. Dickie, determined to have his run, and confident that these youths were not to be feared, picked up a little speed and busted through their barrier, whereupon they all scattered, surprised. This certainly illustrates his determination to not let anything get in the way of his daily run!

Many athletes are frequently waylaid with injuries over their sporting careers, and this can put a barrier in the way of persistent performance. Dickie has had some occasional injuries but looking back, he realized he had run forty years with no major injuries. After the age of sixty, he began to be bothered by calcium deposits in his heels, lungs, and arteries, but it certainly has not stopped him. He runs every day and races every weekend when the races are on. Apart from the calcium deposits, he has had a pulled hamstring, a pulled IT band, compartment syndrome and fasciotomy surgery, a ruptured Achilles tendon and surgery on both feet, carotid artery surgery, with 90% blockage on the left side, basal cell carcinoma surgery, sciatica treatments, and the removal of scar tissue from his reinjured Achilles tendon. But in the last six years, no injuries.

Running story three – Mark Rosenberg

I had just finished my six sessions of chemo and hadn't missed one day of running during this time. Sure, I had some really slow runs, but I still knew I wasn't walking because I had to use full breaths and push forward even when I was tried. My heart rate averaged at 155 beats per minute.

Running gave me something to look forward to and a way to measure how my body was being affected by a private little chemical warfare. It is truly a gift.

My doctor said he had only three patients who had run through their chemo treatments, and he felt they all responded the best to the treatment. I'm not sure about why this is so, but I certainly recommend you hold onto your running shoes when you are going through difficult moments in your life. Don't worry about speed—just keep going, one foot after the other, and it will all feel better in the end.[16]

---

[16] Posted on Dickie's Facebook page and shared with writer on 30th Sept 2020 by email.

CHAPTER FOUR

The drive from the beginning

Longo, Dickie – Running Pic from 'The Times' 2017. Sourced on FB.

It was around twenty-five years ago, that Dickie started to run competitively in road races. He credits his initial motivation to a conversation with his neighbor, a member of the New Orleans Track Club, who had seen him running locally. The neighbor suggested Dickie compete in some of the club's races, and after an initial hesitation, Dickie agreed to do it. "I told him I was afraid I would come in last, but he kept encouraging me," Dickie stated when interviewed by a local newspaper a few years ago. His first official running race entry was the Audubon Trace 5K in New Orleans, where he proved himself wrong and came in first in his age group. After the race, Dickie realized how much he had enjoyed it, especially that lovely feeling of having a win! [17]

---

[17] Hodges, Earl, 2017, *The Times – Picayune*.

The New Orleans Track Club (NOTC) is a membership organization composed of and administered by runners and walkers, and their mission is to "produce and promote running events both as a competitive sport and as one of the best athletic activities for achieving physical and mental fitness." He also belongs to the NOLA Running Systems racing club. Both New Orleans Track Club and NOLA Running Systems racing club conduct very well-organized races in the area. Dickie also belongs to the Chalmette Track Club and the Gulf Coast Running Club and runs for the Atlanta Track Club in National Masters Track Meets.

[18]A quick glance at the results board on the New Orleans Track Club website, brings up ten races in which Dickie has won the over-eighty-age group in 2019 and 2020. The club is community-spirited, with membership dues partly contributing to the running of programs such as "Youth Run NOLA" and "Girls on the Run," which aim to encouraged the youth in the city to begin their lives with a healthy lifestyle, and change lives for the better. [19] Girls on the Run International, for example, is a positive development program that was founded in 1996 in Charlotte, North Carolina, for girls third through to eighth grade, that combines running with interactive group activities, culminating in a 5k race in which the girls, their coaches, family, and friends all participate. Through the program, the girls learn how to set goals, develop self-respect, and make healthy choices. [20] One of the participants was quoted as saying "I learned that anything is possible because I ran a 5k."

Dickie himself has reviewed the New Orleans Track Club highly. He wrote on their Facebook page in 2019, "Great race director. Wonderful food, wonderful group of runners." His words reflect his attitude in life, one of gratitude and appreciation as well as his love of and respect for his running club. Dickie's friend, Allan Robertson, also reviewed the club in a positive light, writing "Great club. Well run races and grand prix. I drive fifty miles to do their races instead of local races. These guys are great!"[21] In fact, there are many positive reviews of the club, and the joy that is felt by the members is evident in the photos on the page.

---

[18] New Orleans Track Club, Inc. https://runnotc.org/index.shtml viewed 13-04-20
[19] As above
[20] New Orleans Track Club Newsletter, 2009-2010, https://runnotc.org/footprints/fp-2010-0102.pdf, viewed 13-04-20
[21] New Orleans Track Club, Inc, Facebook Page, https://www.facebook.com/pg/runNOTC/reviews/?ref=page_internal , viewed 13-04-20

These display moments of the many races they hold each year, many of which are themed in appealing ways, such as "The Greek Fest Run and Walk" and the "Mardi Gras 5k." This club certainly seems to know how to make running fun for everyone! In 2009, New Orleans Mayor-Elect Mitch Landrieu was quoted as saying, "every city has its own attractions, but New Orleans is an attraction unto itself. I would expect people would like to come here." This rather humble statement was made after he finished his inaugural Mardi Gras half marathon, displaying that the races are part of the very visceral system of the city.[22]

Dickie continued with the club, and he has made a positive impression on many other club members. For example, Jim Marsalis, from Old Jefferson, was in graduate school at Tulane when Dickie, who he knew as "Coach Longo," coached basketball there. Marsalis, who was seventy-two at the time, described being "impressed and inspired by Coach Longo's accomplishments in the weekly races, and his ability to maintain a healthy body and spirit week after week."[23]

Dickie's joy in running is contagious. He has about six thousand friends on his Facebook page at the time of writing, many of whom enjoy interacting with his regular posts and updates.

In a normal year, Dickie aims to race every Saturday, in races ranging from the "power mile," two-mile, four-mile, 5k, 8k, 10k, and 12k. He has kept to a strict training schedule for many years. In September 2017, Dickie described his training schedule on his Facebook page, as: Monday five miles, Tuesday four miles, Wednesday HIIT (intervals at 200 meters), Thursday hill runs and Friday two miles. Saturday he will race and then another three miles on Sunday. In 2019 Dickie's running stats were 1280 miles, 54 races, 46 races won in his 80+ age group and he had raced in seven states.

Since 2008 (at time of writing) he has won races in his age groups 371 times and he has a goal of 500 races to win by the age of eighty-five. Despite COVID-19, which has afflicted and killed many in the USA as well as other countries, Dickie continues to run, despite the obvious risk to his own health (though he has been practicing social distancing and wearing a facemask) and he has continued clocking up the miles. A friend of Dickie's checked his world ranking in

---

[22] New Orleans Track Club Newsletter, 2009-2010, https://runnotc.org/footprints/fp-2010-0102.pdf, viewed 13-04-20

[23] Hodges, Earl, 2017, *The Times – Picayune*.

February 2020, and stated that Dickie ranked in the top 32% in the world in his age group and the top 20% in USA. Dickie advises other runners to run forty miles a month (64.374 km) and enter one race. He believes this gives us a reason to go and train to get ready for that monthly race and he has found that this is a strong motivation during the week to get in that regular training.

Dickie was invited to have some free beer after a race, (no doubt, it would not have been the first invitation!) He declined, telling his friend, "I don't drink beer and never have." He recalls the story of when he was a freshman high school quarterback, his coach told him, "you want to be all-state someday, you have to follow these rules. No alcohol, beer, wine, coffee, tea. Bed by 9:00 P.M." Dickie was okay with this, as at the time he had to get up early for his morning paper route anyway. So, he always said no to cigarettes, cigars, and dope. To this day, Dickie has continued to avoid all of them, instead indulging in a hot chocolate made with baking chocolate, half skim milk, half water, and Truvia (a sugar alternative popular in the USA).

Dickie sticks to his healthy regime, no drinking, no smoking, a pescatarian diet (largely based on vegetables and fish), and regular eight hours of sleep per night. At the start of 2020 he was diagnosed with some liver spots, and his doctor told him, "you have had too many birthdays." Dickie's advice to others? "So, my friends, stop having birthdays."

Running Story Four – Leon Gray

A little over nine years ago, I was doing a little cross training on my bike. At a crosswalk, I collided with a bus for the disabled, breaking the windshield and resulting in me being airlifted to the local trauma hospital. I don't remember any of it, which is kind of sad, as it was my first and only ride in a helicopter! The damage I incurred included a shattered hip, a broken leg, and various other fractures, and I ended up in a coma for two months. When I woke from the coma, my wife happened to be there and she told me that the first thing I said was "I love you!" Was I lucky!

My quick recovery after the accident has been accredited to me being an ultra-trail runner, and at the age of sixty-four being in excellent condition.

About six months later, I was recovering well and walking regularly, when unfortunately, I developed a hernia and a hematoma, leading to a hospital stay in which I contracted MSRA. These things stretched my recovery out to two years, after which, with the legal issues finally settled, I began to enter 5k races. My first 5k took me forty-five minutes—a length that used to take me around twenty-three minutes before my accident.But I persisted, until eventually I completed in a twenty-six-mile race that I did in twelve hours, finishing the race with world-class blisters, which took several months to heal.

Several months later, I competed in a 30k trail race and right at the finish I was trying to beat an eighty-year-old lady, when about thirty feet from the finish line, I did an epic face-plant onto asphalt. There were rumours that I had been tripped, but I think it more likely my own feet and maybe a speed bump got in the way. This ended up with a trip to the ER, but there was nothing more serious than a bloody face. At the coffee shop later, the guy behind the counter asked if I needed an ambulance—to which my daughter replied we had just come from the hospital, and all was fine.

After that, I did several 5ks and got my time down to 11:08 pace, which made me happy.In 2016 the wheels came off,though, with PF, hamstring, and knee and it took me one and a half years before I felt like doing anything again. In 2018, though, I was back, competing in three ultras with a 50k and two and two twelve hour runs of about thirty-four miles. 2019 saw me competing in seven races, with the best being a 100km race, which took about twenty-five hours to finish.

I have been inspired reading Dickie's stories on his Facebook page, and I wish him all the best, with his story and his scholarship Fund. I might mention, while I was in the local hospital, a bunch of running friends decided to run by the hospital and say hi, even though I was still in a coma.The nurses would only let five people in at a time so twenty-five or more runners had to wait their turn! [24]

---

[24] Leon Gray, April 2020, sent to writer by email.

CHAPTER FIVE

Powered by faith and love–
Dickie's keys to success

When corresponding with Dickie, what stands out more clearly than anything else, and often makes an appearance in his stories, is his love of his wife Beverley. Dickie credits Beverley as being the inspiration of his running passion, his "running muse," as it were.

"My wife was and still is beautiful," he wrote. "She has a great figure, and I asked myself, 'what can I do to keep up with her?' which led to me taking up running." Beverley is also active; she swims and walks, and Dickie speaks proudly of them both being the same weight now as when they married. A favourite quote I have of Dickie's is "I really out-married myself, but don't tell her."

When Dickie was a "pretty good high school athlete," (a description,of course, highly underplaying his athletic ability, given that he lettered in four sports), he had an experience outside of the sporting arena, that was going to come in handy later on. Senior English wasn't his strength, he admitted, and concerned that his lowish marks in the subject might affect his chances of being eligible for all of his four sports that he loved, Dickie asked his teacher how he could bring up his grade. Her suggestion was to memorize a poem and recite it to his English class. The poem he was assigned was "How do I love thee" by Elizabeth Barrett Browning. Initially, Dickie proclaimed in horror, "No, I am an athlete, we don't recite love poems!"

Truthfully, though, Dickie was keen on a challenge, and he went ahead and memorized the poem, and found himself in front of his English class, ready to recite it. After the first two lines, he went blank and he began to think he had no chance of recalling the poem—perhaps his chances of staying in his chosen sports were doomed! But luckily, the lines came back, and he recited the whole poem, (ending with a bow to the class and a standing ovation!) and in so doing, Dickie raised his English grade enough to keep playing the sports for which he had so much passion.

Somehow this must have been part of his life plan, because while he was at college, he first saw Beverley, who he describes as "the prettiest girl I have ever seen." Unfortunately, she wasn't quite as interested in him as he was her, and she refused his first request for a date. Beverley then continued to refuse Dickie's repeated displays of affection for three years, until in senior year, she finally agreed to a date. (Nobody can say that he is not persistent in reaching for his goals, that is for certain).

Things went well on this long-awaited occasion and Dickie fell madly in love. Not too long after they had begun dating, Dickie decided the time was right.

One night, he began to recite the words of the poem he had learned in class:

<blockquote>
I love thee to the depth and breadth and height
My soul can reach, when feeling out of sight
For the ends of being and ideal grace.
I love thee to the level of every day's
Most quiet need, by sun and candle-light.
I love thee freely, as men strive for right.
I love thee purely, as they turn from praise.
I love thee with the passion put to use
In my old griefs, and with my childhood's faith.
I love thee with a love I seemed to lose
With my lost saints. I love thee with the breath,
Smiles, tears, of all my life; and, if God choose,
I shall but love thee better after death.' [25]
</blockquote>

And after this display of true love, what was Beverley's reply, but, "That sure is corny!"

Dickie was not taken aback, instead adding the words,

"By the way, will you marry me?"

---

[25] Forward Arts Foundation, 'National Poetry Day,' https://nationalpoetryday.co.uk/poem/how-do-i-love-thee-sonnet-43/, viewed 17-05-20

Of course, the answer was yes. Dickie stated, with a twinkle in the eye, "I really out-married myself, but don't tell her."Beverley herself will only add,"It has been a good and happy marriage."

Dickie's Facebook posts often mention the love of his life, and while he has a never-ending passion for taking on new challenges, Beverley is always there in the background, his supporter and also his moderator. For example, Dickie was describing in a post on the 10th of August, 2019, that he had run a 5k race, and had finished up right with no falls. He was a bit disappointed with his time and mentioned it to Beverley when he got home, feeling that his slower time was due to getting older and his knee hurting from a fall the previous week. Beverley replied, "Don't give me excuses, just get your butt out there and run!"

Don't we all need someone to tell us that occasionally?

Beverley has also been responsible for making sure that Dickie doesn't become too obsessed with running and athletics, and through her encouragement he has enjoyed many cultural experiences over his lifetime. For example, on August 14, 2019. Dickie wrote about a trip they were taking to the Chautauqua Institute for a week, stating,"my wife thinks I need more culture and less running. I will attend lectures, symphony, ballet, ensembles, and group discussion. We will have good entertainment each evening like the Beach Boys, Melissa Etheridge, Three Tenors, and others. I will however, get to run two 5k races, 'something I want to do'—both have an 80+ division award winner."

"When I return," he wrote, "I will be full of culture and have two winners medals. It's a wonderful life." Somehow Dickie has been able to combine his passion and love of running with his passion and love of Beverley, for more than sixty years!

In April 2020, Dickie and Beverley celebrated their sixtieth wedding anniversary. To commemorate this, Dickie decided to run sixty laps around the football field at the Playground, and then take Beverley out with some friends to get some charbroiled oysters Cajun style. He reflected, "Hard to believe my lovely wife has put up with this old runner for sixty years. Long suffering, I guess." When he posted a picture of them in their early years of marriage, someone asked Dickie their ages. Dickie would not reveal Beverley's age, but told them they were twenty-two when they married.

During their early years of marriage, Dickie took his first position as a teacher and assistant basketball coach at Tulane University, and they moved six times in seven years. Eventually Beverley insisted "no more moving," and they haven't moved since. They have now lived in New Orleans for fifty-two years, and they bought a condo in Fort Myers, Florida, where their son Reed and his family lives, and occasionally the couple "move" there for a few weeks of rest and relaxation.

Beverley tolerates her husband's running habit, or his "vice," as he calls it, although she isn't particularly keen on his 4:00 A.M. rises when he has to drive to a race somewhere. She puts up with it, though, just as Dickie accepts and supports Beverley's "vices" of book club, two bridge clubs, church women's club, and volunteering. Both really enjoy being active members of the community, and this has also helped them remain the happy and committed couple they are today.

On May 22, 2020, there were three deaths of people who had attended Dickie and Beverley's church. Their ages were eighty-three, eight-four, and eighty-nine. Dickie went to the grocery store with Beverley and he wrote the following:

"I went to grocery with a list my wife gave me and bought a lot of groceries. Came home with them and my angel wife went to work. She cooked about four meals for each of the families. She worked all day cooking, what a warrior! We then delivered them to all families."

Dickie's descriptions of Beverley are always filled with love and respect.

Dickie and Beverley still love to dance when they go out to social events. Dickie says, "being so old we are usually the hit at wedding receptions dancing, we can really move!"

Apart from Dickie's love of his wife, and entwined and interweaved with it, is Dickie's faith in God. Dickie's faith and his running are intermingled. He has attended church with Beverley regularly, and while not always hugely enthusiastic about church itself,and still making his running more of a priority (for example, when he arrived at halftime wearing his running warmup suit in October 2019), his faith in the God he believes in comes through many of his writings.

Dickie wrote in June 2019, "I have to race as much as possible at age 82, with what time I have left. Before long I will be running the Heaven 5k. I will win the 80+ but Jesus will win the 2000+."

Dickie's running routine can almost be interpreted as a form of prayer. He runs for an hour a day, broken into twenty-minute segments. In the first twenty minutes, he reflects on his day and the actions he has taken within it. He notes any mistakes he has made and focuses on any areas he needs to improve. In the next twenty minutes, he plans for the next day, and focuses on how he can be more helpful and a better runner. And the final twenty minutes, are spent thanking God for all his blessings, for allowing him to run and for sending prayer requests of safety for those he knows, family, and friends. He also asks for forgiveness. Dickie runs all races in God's honor and tells him this too.

Does he pray to win a race? Dickie is adamant that he does not pray to win, but to run to his full potential, whatever that may be. He is aware that every runner's potential is different. One special prayer that Dickie says every year on January 1st, is a thank-you to God for allowing him to run the races that he has,and then a prayer request to run races in the coming year, if it is his will. He has welcomed in the new year with the same prayer for twenty-two years. "Prayer is powerful," he writes. "It gets me through a race very time. Ask and you will receive. Amen."

Dickie recalls his prayer life starting many years ago when he was a teenager. His mother had walked out, and his dad was working all the time, and Dickie would lie in his bed, sweating, with no air conditioner. To distract him from the discomfort, he would talk to God. He would tell him about his day, ask for his help for the next and thank him for getting him and his family through another day safely. He would then listen for a response and fall asleep. "I guess he talked back. I was most comfortable when talking with him."

Dickie's sense of thankfulness shines through all he does and all he says. He describes himself as "the most blessed man on the face of the earth and thus always happy." He is proud of his family and his life in general. "Great wife, great sons, great grandchildren, great friends, great church, great running groups, great health, great mission to help others. To this point I have had the best life of anyone anywhere. God is good all the time, to me."

Reflecting on his life in his later years, Dickie's gratitude towards the joy and success he had experienced inspired him to "pay it back," a decision he made without much fanfare. Valuing the power of running in his life and knowing that the humble activity has the potential to improve the lives of so many, Dickie decided to make it his mission to help as many people as he could. This began by giving running shoes to those who needed them and paying entry fees to running races, for those who could not afford them.

He also gave away running outfits to many people and soon expanded his mission to include meeting other needs of people in the community, such as money to pay for a funeral, money, clothes, and shoes for homeless veterans and financial support to buy musical instrumentsor college textbooks, things that have real potential to lift people up to a better life outcome. Dickie decided to create his Longo Scholarship Fund, to bring together what had so far been an "ad-hoc" approach to giving in the community, and although he had retired, this new inspiration motivated him to return to work, all with the aim of raising money to help others through the fund.

Dickie's reflections on his Facebook page often demonstrate his faith in God, a quiet and steadfast faith that is the anchor to his excellent character and generosity.

After a post in which he wrote of giving his own shoes to a teenage boy in need, he wrote the following: "I think maybe God has a hand in this. I feel he is sending me to places to help people save their lives with running. Could that be possible? I feel like I am a running missionary."

Dickie has a strong sense that God places him where he needs to be at the right time. For example, there was an incident when he normally ran at the park on Wednesdays every week, but for once there was a board meeting on the Wednesday, so he swapped his run to a Thursday. On that Thursday, he met the young mother who he inspired to run again (see the next chapter), and he feels that perhaps it was God's plan or part of his mission, perhaps both of them were sent there to run together.

Running story five – Joyce Riley

Joyce's story reflects how reading Dickie's stories and seeing his kindness has inspired her to do the same.

I had a tough, heat-filled ten-mile run/walk today, but while I was out there, I saw a family out trail-riding on their bikes. They were resting in the shade and looked a bit stressed. I stopped and asked them if they were okay. The wife was struggling with the heat, which was at the time sitting at 97 degrees (Fahrenheit). I warned them that the water fountains are turned off farther up the trail, and to make sure they were prepared with water. On my way back to my car, I was very low on water and with three miles left, so when they passed me, they asked if I was okay.

I said, "I am low on water but going to walk back to my car." They stopped in front of me and dropped a full bottle of water for me, being careful to social distance due to the COVID-19 pandemic. That bottle of water really helped me the last three miles. Your inspiration of caring about people (Dickie Longo), has made me more aware of people on the trail and today that caring on my part came back with these trail angels—a perfect illustration of how kindness is contagious. Thank you!

Hardworking man –
from delivery boy to rocket man

For a man who loves to set himself goals and run every day, racing each weekend wherever possible, it is not surprising to learn that this determination to work hard has been present from an early age. Dickie's first job was to deliver the local newspaper. He was ten years old and his paper route would start at 4:00 A.M., when he would get himself out of bed and run to the store to pick up his packs of papers to be delivered. For a while, he was able to deliver the papers on his bike, but when his bike broke, it was back to the on-foot delivery. Many miles were run in the name of "employment."

After he returned from his paper route, Dickie would wake his brother Bob, help him get dressed, fix breakfast for them both and then walk with him to school. With his Dad working all night and sleep all day and his mother having left the family home some time ago, Dickie found himself largely responsible for his brother's welfare. On the way home, he and Bob would stop at the playground, encouraged by a playground director who was keen on running. He made everyone there run laps and sprints around many blocks, which Dickie reflects was teaching them discipline. After training, Dickie would walk home with Bob and fix dinner, do his homework and go to bed, only to get up again at 4am to restart the routine. Dickie credits this disciplined lifestyle as keeping him on track, as there was no opportunity to get into 'real trouble' with such a demanding schedule.

The paper route was a five-year stint, from the ages of ten to fifteen, and his best friend, three doors up, also had a paper route. He and his friend wanted to try out for the Freshman football team, and as they could not access a gym to build their strength, they decided to make their own barbells. This was quite an adventure! They wandered to a house construction site and watched the builders mixing concrete in an old concrete mixer, and then copied them by filling two empty gallon paint cans and putting an iron bar between them, sticking the cans on each end, thus creating a perfect barbell. Taking turns lifting their ingenious home-made barbell, the boys managed to gain enough strength to make the varsity football team, and Dickie, as a freshman, was excited to join the team as a quarterback.

During this time, Dickie was able to save his earnings and purchase a used Cushman motor scooter, an achievement of which he is proud. He also has a funny story of when he was doing his paper round. At this time, he was running from house to house delivering papers, and on Saturday afternoons would go to every house to collect his weekly payment. Many times, no one would be home, or they wouldn't answer the doorbell. He had to collect enough money to pay the paper bill to his supervisor. Many times, after paying this, he would only have about two dollars left.

On one such occasion, when he knocked on the door of one of his customers, a young lady of around eighteen answered. She asked him to come and sit down while she got the money, then returned and sat right next to Dickie on a big sofa and began to engage in small talk. When she started rubbing his hand, he realized something wasn't right, and bounced up out of the sofa, sprinted down the hallway and out of the front door, running down the block as fast as he could. After that, her papers were delivered, but he never went back to collect a fee—she scored a free paper from then on in. Dickie's reflection on the incident? "Just another example where running saved this scared boy!"

At high school, Dickie's athleticism had come into its own. He lettered in four sports, football, basketball, baseball, and track. In Spring, he would alternate between baseball one day and track the next. In 1955, you didn't need to be built like a house to play sports, so Dickie's lean frame was perfectly suited. Dickie was successful in obtaining a full basketball and baseball scholarship to a small NAIA college, Transylvania University, in Lexington, Kentucky.

After the paper route, Dickie began to help his father in his used-car lot, where he would work on cars. On the first Saturday of the month, the three of them would drive to a car auction in a town about sixty miles away, where they would bid on cars to buy for their used car lot. He would then drive back home in one of the cars they had bought. Sometimes they purchased two or three cars, so on those days, Dickie would then drive back to the auction site with his dad and drive home another of the cars. Most of his Saturdays were spent doing this. In those days (1950), the cars were American made (foreign cars were not available for them to sell), and included Ford, Chevrolet, Buick, and Pontiacs amongst others. Dickie's tasks also included washing and polishing each car, waiting on customers, and taking them on test-drives, as well as doing minor repairs.

Dickie's working relationship with his father was strained, as he really didn't want to be there, and it was certainly no secret. The fact that he was never paid for his work was the main reason why he felt so resentful. Reflecting on the situation now, Dickie realizes that his father could not afford to pay him anything and he is more understanding, but in those days, from the perspective of an adolescent boy developing his independence, it felt very unfair. For a long time though, every Saturday, he would help his father, and get up early to go to work after a hard ball game on the Friday night, with no financial reward.

After he graduated from high school, Dickie was accepted into college, and he excitedly ran to his father to break the news. Expecting to be congratulated, it came as a huge blow when his father was far from impressed, and instead refused to support him, insisting that he needed his help at the car lot and could not do without him. Dickie had a dilemma on his hands, as he loved his father and his brother, and felt torn between staying to assist and leaving to follow his dreams.

But in his heart of hearts, he knew that this life of selling cars was not for him, and he had so much more to offer, and in a few weeks after receiving the offer to college (with a full scholarship based on his athletic ability and achievements), he packed up his little suitcase with the few clothes he owned and snuck out of the house, hitchhiking to the place where he would spend the next few years. He had a vision for himself, and it wasn't one that involved working in a used car-lot for the rest of his life!

Out of the jobs he has done, Dickie recalls his time as basketball coach at Tulane University most fondly. He became head basketball coach in 1971. The season opened in early December and the first game was against a top ten opponent—the University of Wisconsin. Knowing it was really cold there, he had his team practice running for hours with steam heaters fully turned on and when it came to the game, he turned up the heaters, then watched Wisconsin literally fade in the second half of the game. Dickie still gets Christmas cards from former players, thanking him for motivating them to run, many of them are still running in their fifties.

1971-1972 Photo of Dick Longo in Tulane University Brochure.

After Dickie left coaching in the early 1970s, he began working as a textbook sales consultant. Other positions he has held, include Consultant for the Physical Fitness Institute of America. Some of the jobs were when he was still in school, but looking back, Dickie is proud of the various jobs he has taken during his life-time, explaining 'They say variety is the spice of life, so I am pretty spicy!' Today, Dickie speaks highly of his work in the Longo Scholarship Fund, a personal philanthropic endeavor, where he is helping others in purchasing or acquiring (through his generosity), running shoes, entry fees and funds for homeless veterans and others.

Dickie describes his position as Co-director of the Physical Fitness Institute of America in the 1970s as another highlight. The role involved developing a fitness program that the Apollo astronauts used while travelling in space, which consisted of using a small resistant device that could be used effectively in weightlessness. The astronauts were so pleased with the program that it was then promoted primarily to business executives throughout the USA, and Dickie was involved with the creation and promotion of the Apollo Exerciser.

According to an article in the Smithsonian, [26] Apollo 7 was the first-time astronauts had enough room to exercise, and in preparation for the flight, NASA experts sought an inflight exerciser that was small and lightweight. This led to the development of the "Exer-Genie Exerciser" in 1961 by Exer-Genie Inc, of Fullerton California. This was a variable resistance rope friction device which was originally designed to lower people from a burning building and was adapted to a small exercise machine and given its market name. The Exer-Genie was carried on every crewed Apollo mission and used on Apollo missions 7, 8, 9, 11, 12 and 16 and later, Skylab. Astronauts would typically use it every day for fifteen to thirty minutes while in the command module. After the Apollo 11 mission, Neil Armstrong stated that they did a little bit of exercise almost every day. He is quoted as saying, 'The Exer-Genie worked alright. It got a little hot and stored a lot of heat, but it was acceptable.'[27] The original model continues to be adapted and marketed under different names and has been quite a success. [28] Dickie's team eventually built on the concept of this early device and created the Apollo Exerciser, which was reportedly easier to use.

So, while Dickie did not stay on in the car sales yard with his father and brother, he did carry out his father's strong work ethic and has continued to earn money in a wide array of positions throughout his lifetime. Some other positions he held include one painting letters on top of an airplane hangar, one where he was hand digging footing for a new hotel on a beach, a playground director, truck driver, a painter of college dorm rooms and the driver of a school bus. He was also the bus-boy for the YWCA, a teacher, an assistant, and head basketball coach in high school as well as community park director, a tobacco field surveyor and laborer, a baseball umpire, youth community action director, fact book sales rep and an extra in movies!

[26] Smithsonian National Air and Space Museum website, 07/01/2016, viewed 31st May 2020, https://airandspace.si.edu/stories/editorial/apollo-inflight-exerciser
[27] Brain Pile Blog, viewed 07/06/2020, https://brainpile.wordpress.com/2012/08/07/the-apollo-exerciser/
[28] Exergenie Website, viewed 0/06/2020, https://www.exergenie.com/

Dickie's work life has of course had its challenges. When Hurricane Katrina hit New Orleans in August 2005 (one of the deadliest hurricanes to ever hit the United States, with the loss of 1,833 people in the hurricane and the flooding that followed),[29] Dickie lost his job. Luckily, he found another one eventually, and began delivering lost luggage from the airport to its rightful owners. It would frequently happen that on each flight, a few passengers would find that their luggage was not on the plane, and it usually arrived the next day or so. Dickie would go to the airport in the morning and load up the found luggage, then deliver it to the homes of the owners.

On one occasion, Dickie delivered a lady's luggage, and when she opened the door, she stated, "my prayer is answered!" Her husband was in bed sick as he had not had his medication for forty-eight hours, as it was in the missing luggage. Dickie disappeared before she had the chance to give him a tip and he is certain that God put him in the right place at the right time to assist this ailing man. This is one of the many times where Dickie can clearly see a connection between his relationship with God and the events in his life, as mentioned earlier.

When he was sixty-five, he advised Earl Hodges, (journalist for the *Times-Picayune*) [30] he retired for a total of six months but grew restless and wanted to get back to work. "I love working and running," Dickie was quoted as stating, and at eighty-three (at time of writing), this has certainly not changed.

Running story six – Joseph Warren

I started running around 1969. I was in junior high school and read an abbreviated version of Ken Cooper's book, *Aerobics* in the *Readers Digest*. I was a husky kid and thought that jogging would keep me in shape. I got more serious about running when I got involved in martial arts and running became a great way for me to keep my weight down and stay in shape for tournaments. I also

---

[29] Live Science, viewed 07/06/2020 https://www.livescience.com/22522-hurricane-katrina-facts.html#:~:text=Hurricane%20Katrina%20was%20one%20of,Coast%20and%20in%20New%20Orleans.

[30] Hodges, Earl 'Dick Longo, 80, still enjoys the thrill of racing against others,' *The Times – Picayune*, 16/07/2017

played football and threw the shotput on the Track and Field. I continued to run in college and graduate school, along with swimming and weightlifting.

I ran my first race in 1980, The Crescent City Classic 10k in New Orleans. That is when I really fell in love with running and the running community in New Orleans. I ran my first marathon in 1982, the Mardi Gras Marathon. Running has been an indispensable part of my life since. I have no idea how many races I have run. Distances from 100 meters to 50k. I have run eighteen marathons, one ultramarathon and fifty triathlons. My PRs are respectable for someone my size and my best Marathon time is 3:34:04, PB for 10k is 41:19, for 4k 19:32 and two mile: 19.32.

I still run four to six days with mileage between twenty to thirty miles per week, though I also walk as well. I am sixty-four years old. I still do some light weights and bike a couple of days a week. Unfortunately, I have osteoarthritis in my shoulders and can no longer swim.

To me running means developing lifelong friendship with some great people. It also has left me with wonderful memories (the seventies and eighties really did rock!).I have had many encounters with people who stop me when I am running, or in a restaurant or grocery shopping and tell me how they see me running for years and thank me for giving them incentive. One woman even said it was my ministry! Another man, who is overweight has been waving and talking to me whenever I passed his house. One day he asked my age and I told him. I was older than him. The next time I saw him, he looked surprisingly good. He told me I inspired him to start walking. He now walks five miles a day and has dropped fifteen pounds. I plan on doing my best to keep putting one foot in front of the other for as long as God lets me.

Fatherhood - how a good man lives on through his family

Dickie and Beverley have three sons. Reed is the eldest, with his name chosen as it is Beverley's middle name. The second was Rob, named after Dickie's brother. After their third son was named Ross, Dickie joked that if they had another son he would have to be named "Redundant" or "Ridiculous"; however a fourth child was not to be (fortunately, perhaps, if he were going to be named those names!)

Dickie recalled that when his second son, Rob, was about three years old, he would read him a bedtime story and after the story, he would say his prayers. After the prayers, Dickie would tell him that he loved him very much. Rob would answer, "I love you a hundred times," Dickie would say, "I love you a million times," Rob would reply, "I love you a billion," and Dickie would respond, "I love you a trillion times." Rob would think and say, "Daddy, I love you till there are no more numbers!"

Reed Longo – recollections

Reed is the eldest of Dickie's three sons. He lives in Fort Myers, Florida, with his wife Cindy and three children, Ryan, Mia, and Callie. The couple owns and operates a facility on thirty acres, called "Golf World," which includes a retail strip center and a full golf practice range and Pro shop. Reed shared some of his recollections of his father. Reed remembers his father when he was a highly ranked national tennis player, before he fell in love with running. He described him training for his tennis matches by running different distances and speed intervals and believes that initially his father only ran to get in shape for tennis, but slowly decided he would prefer to run a 5k race on Saturday morning than spend his whole weekend travelling and then playing four to five tennis matches over a two-day period.

Reed was a Division One college tennis player at the University of Southern Mississippi and was introduced to the game by his father. Dickie and Reed would train for hours at their local club, and Dickie would stay and practice with Reed if he needed, never complaining. Once they qualified to play in a father and son doubles tennis tournament hosted at the US Open Site in New York. They qualified along with sixteen other teams from around the country. Reed described this as a great bonding and competitive experience for a father and son, as they had to advance across some extraordinarily strong teams from the entire South region. Unfortunately, Dickie had a bad pinched nerve in his neck and could barely move his head, causing them to lose, however Reed remembers the real prize being getting to play their match on Court Sixteen on the US Open grounds and attend all the pro matches.

A memory from an earlier period was when Reed was playing doubles tennis with his partner Rick Teissier in a junior tennis tournament in Lafayette, Louisiana when he was fourteen years old. Dickie would take them to the tournaments and watch most of their matches unless it interfered with his afternoon training run. Rick recalls an extremely hot late summer day when the temperature was approximately ninety-five degrees Fahrenheit, (35 C) with an extremely high humidity which made it almost unbearable. They were playing their match and Dickie was running around the entire tennis complex, over and over for approximately an hour or more. Other parents and players were in the shade and still suffering from the heat and were wondering if perhaps this man had a mental health condition. Reed and Rick told them, "no, that's just Dick Longo on his afternoon training mission." Reed remembers being proud of his father that day, and on many other days when his training and work ethic inspired him to train longer and harder to achieve his own personal goals.

Reed describes his father as a big motivation and inspiration to both his family and to many friends and new acquaintances he meets. He says he always "goes the extra mile, no pun intended," to help those who are willing to try to better and help themselves and that he gives those people optimism and hope moving forward.

Rob Longo – recollections

Rob's recollection of his childhood is a positive one, with many of his memories focused on his dad's sporting interests and career. Rob also speaks of his mother's influence as a "softener," and that the balance between his parents worked well. Rob recalls moving from Indiana to New Orleans at a young age, where his father was coaching the Tulane Basketball team (as assistant then head coach) in his early thirties. He recalls being driven around in the family's Volkswagen Beetle (a car which he still loves), and he recalls the basketball games and the excitement of being on the bench at the arena.

While his dad evidently loved coaching, Rob recalled, he left the job because it was not conducive to family life, with the constant need to be at games, or recruiting, holding camps,and conducting fundraising activities. It also involved teaching a class, which his father was a natural at, being a teacher. Rob also recalls the racism which was evident in the community of New Orleans at the time and remembers having some boys stay with them for a Tulane summer camp. He recalled that some of the folks on their block made it known that they did not like the color of their skin. Rob recalls his father standing up for these boys, and many other boys as well, and describes him as having a "great moral compass."

Rob believes that his father's passion for sports grew out of his escape from a tough life growing up. One way out of that place was to excel in sports, by outworking everyone else, and he also believes that his dad was naturally competitive. Sports provided an outlet where he could challenge himself to the full against other athletes. Rob also believes his dad was tough, and stated, "he would stand up to anybody, and call people out who were doing something he did not think was right." This sometimes created a situation where Rob would worry that it would not turn out well, but luckily it always worked out, as he was able to convey to others what the "right thing to do" was.

One of the sports Rob recalls his father playing, is competitive tennis, and what stood out was his attitude. Dickie would say,"I might not be the best player or have the most talent, but they are not going to outlast me on the court." It was a lesson that Rob took with him, into other areas of life. Rob stated that at law school, he wasn't the smartest in the class, but he had the 'street smarts' to out-work others. He now also gives this advice to his daughters, who are growing up in a hyper competitive and visible time. "There may be someone who has a higher IQ or other advantage than you, but don't compare yourself to them, just do your own thing with your God-given gifts. Compete with them, outwork them, stay in the battle and be firm and tough." As he hears his own advice to his girls, Rob also hears his father's advice coming through, and recognizes what an influence he has been.

Rob recalls that after his father left basketball coaching, he became a referee, which allowed him to be close to the game and get paid to exercise. He was also the University of New Orleans Tennis Coach, and still wears the silver ring proudly. This, Rob believes, displays how hard his father worked, probably harder than any of his competitors, but he is also aware that you need natural talent to get that far in sports and coaching. So, while he couldn't control his challenging childhood circumstances, Dickie found that he could control his sporting prowess to a much higher degree.

Rob says that his mother, Beverley, was just as important to him as his father, and that she guided him and his brothers on the home front, helping them with their studies, taking them to museums and exposing them to literature and history. Church was always a mainstay in the family, and his mother was heavily involved in the church, often staying late after the service, and probably taking advantage of the opportunity to talk about something other than sport! He recalls rushing out of church to get into the car as soon as the sermon ended, to listen to their favorite football team play on the car radio, and his Mom would come out after what seemed forever. His father was also very actively involved in the church, in leadership and fundraising, and he had a great way with words as a public speaker. Rob described him as "having a deep well from which he could just pull something out whenever he needs it,"a sermon, prayer before a meal, or whatever was required, and he describes his daughters as being mesmerized by this ability.

A standout for Rob is his father's faith in God as well as his self-assurance and clarity of vision. He sees parallels in his dad's passion for sports and his faith, in that his father likes to run alone and play singles tennis, but also likes the shared experience with other runners, such as those who follow him on Facebook and see him at the regular races he enters each weekend. This is like faith, Rob believes, which can be solitary but also enjoyable as a shared experience. Rob says his dad is sure about his running, his faith, his wife, and his family. "I don't think you meet too many people these days," shared Rob, "who are as sure of who they are and their place in the world as my dad."

Rob credits this attitude as one which helps him when things become difficult and that his father's encouragement was part of why he has been successful in the corporate world. A memorable phrase of his dad's is this "all I ever wanted was a nice life and a good family that stayed together." He sees his father as "the poor kid who ran to a better life, and kept on running, certainly getting everything he ever wanted," and finished his reflection with the beautiful words, "And we were lucky enough to get him."

Ross Longo – Recollections

When Ross was in sixth or seventh grade, his class was asked to write about their hero, and he wrote about his dad. To Ross, his father's athletic accomplishments in so many areas were truly remarkable. He was an all-state quarterback in high school, played college football at Florida State (now a big-name school) for a short time, and then played small college basketball and baseball. He also played semi-pro baseball during the summer while he worked. He then became a college basketball head coach at Tulane. Ross thought all of that was remarkable. Ross wrote that his father was and still is a mini celebrity in New Orleans from when he coached at Tulane. People would sometimes see him and call him "Coach." All those athletic accomplishments are impressive, but what Ross likes most about his father is his ability to make what you (others) have done seem hugely impressive and remarkable.

"No one is better at making someone feel like they have accomplished something truly astonishing better than my dad. I thought for a long time that he was just easily impressed, but now that I am a dad, I know that he was guessing low each time to make the announcement more special!He did it to me repeatedly.In fact, if I had done something that I thought was cool and I told someone and they weren't that impressed, I would say "I need to tell my dad about this!"

Ross says that his father will talk to anyone.He talks to strangers in the line at a store.He talks to someone when he sees an interesting logo on their shirt, etc and Ross thinks he may have inherited that from his father as well. Ross described his mom as the biggest talker in his family but his dad talks a lot too—"but he has to take his chances to talk whenever he can when he has the chance (because my mom is hard to compete with!)"

"Actually," Ross writes, "all five of us can talk anyone's ear off!" He has a reputation with his own kids as being very chatty.

Ross thinks that if his dad hadn't chosen a career in sales, he should have been a minister.He is great with an audience and in Church services would very often overshadow the minister's sermon with his prayer and readings of the bible.Ross recalls his dad coming to every one of his sporting events, from age five to eighteen, and he thinks this is amazing, describing it as "a hugely impressive feat!" His dad was also there to help him move to a new house each time, until he was thirty-two years old (and his father would have been seventy-one). "He would actually lift everything," Ross wrote. "It was impressive.He still offers to help today (but we just use movers now)."

Ross also recalls that his dad taught him the value of a dollar."I used to go to the movies on Saturday afternoon with friends.The movie would cost $3.25.He would give me $3.00.I would have to find the other $.25 somewhere and I always did.I think this came from his upbringing during WWII and right after.He was thrifty and I am quite thrifty today and credit that to him.My dad raised three very independent boys.They installed in all of us a drive to succeed and do things for yourself.Two of us own our own businesses and the other is a high-level lawyer at a fortune 200 company."

When Ross quit practicing law at the age of twenty-nine, his dad said, "Okay," and was happy for him because he was making a career change and he wanted Ross to be happy.It had not occurred to Ross to go into sales until then and he did, as a commercial real estate broker, and soon after he realised that his dad had been in sales for thirty years and that he was following in his footsteps!

A standout in Ross's memory, is his dad's involvement in both running and tennis, which have been huge parts of his life. He also recalls his dad eating M&Ms and fried chicken a lot when Ross was little, but that did not last long once he really got into running. Ross says that his father is the most recognizable person in their part of Metairie, because everyone sees him running.People would tell him every other day that they saw his dad running.He was everywhere!

Ross finished his account of his father with the following:

"He is a special person.Always optimistic and thinking the glass is half-full.He was always very loving and supportive, and I love him very much."

Kayla Longo – recollections:

Kayla Longo is the granddaughter of Dickie's brother, Bob Longo, who has been a "tremendous father figure" for Kayla, and provided for her as she has grown up, supporting her in all that she has chosen to do. Kayla wrote the following:

While I don't get to see my great uncle very often, I hear about him through my grandfather, Bob, who has been a tremendous father figure for me. My grandfather, and his brother Dickie, have been athletes their entire life and continue to be active today. My grandfather and I had the opportunity to play Division One Golf at Florida Atlantic university. He often tells me about Uncle Dick's accomplishments, and I keep up with him on Facebook.

Once or twice a year, I get to see Uncle Dick and Beverley, and I enjoy catching up with them. For my great uncle to be eighty-three years old and still run the way he does, is motivating. It makes me ask myself, "what's stopping you, Kayla?" Even though I am no longer a student athlete at FAU, my great uncle has shown me that I can be an athlete my entire life. He has made it apparent that you can still enjoy athleticism beyond the college years.

Beyond my great uncle's impressive athleticism and training routine is his devotion to giving back to others. God continues to use Dickie to touch others and it is incredible to see. I can only hope to one day touch the world in half the ways my great uncle has touched it. With his kindness and running miles, I have quite the Longo legacy to carry on. But with my grandfather and Great Uncle being such incredible role models, I am confident that I will make them proud.

Running Story Seven – Janelle Dickerson

How running saved my life

At the age of fifty-five, I have outlived my four siblings. My dad died at the age of fifty-seven, when I was two weeks from graduating from high school in 1984 and my mom passed away at the age of eighty in 2009.Dad drowned in a Reno Casino bathtub. The death certificate says he fell, hit his head, and drowned in a tub full of running water. Mom died from lung disease.

My sister Debbie was born in November 1951. Bruce was born in June 1953. Dan was born in January 1957. I was born in 1965 and Matt was born in 1968. You're supposed to outlive your parents. It's kind of a law or something, at least that's what you're taught growing up. Right? In my family, another kind of law was working against us—the law of attraction to drugs. Drugs were the cause of their early deaths. I could never have predicted being the one who would outlive everyone, just as I'm sure Mom didn't think she'd outlive Matt and Dan.

In 1975, at the age of ten, I started running while attending Sam's Valley Elementary School, Oregon. That same year, Steve Profontaine was tragically killed—the great runner from the small Oregon Coastal town who made it big. I took an interest in running after his tragic death was in the headlines, and my grade schoolteacher noticed the passion I had for it. Fast-forward nine years. I achieved All-American status in track and field, cross-country and competed at state in both sports. I competed in Junior Olympics and my talent earned me tenth place at the cross-country Nationals in Boy's Town, Nebraska in 1983.

In those short nine years, life was not easy. I was put back into pre-primary school and was diagnosed with dyslexia. By the time I was twelve, I had also been sexually molested by three different men, one of whom was a family member. By the time I graduated from high school, I was nineteen and a half.

My parents divorced when I was eight, in 1973, and in that same year, Mom remarried to my stepdad. My dad remarried a few years following my mother's remarriage. Both of my parents and stepparents were heavy drinkers and smokers. Another challenge I faced was that my mom and stepdad didn't hide their sexual activities, and I witnessed them having sex when I was aged eight, an experience that was very traumatizing, especially paired with their heavy drinking and sloppy drunkenness. I dared not bring friends to visit the house.

In 1971 my parents adopted my sister's child, and he was diagnosed with Type 1 diabetes, and his mother died when he was aged only six. He became a drug addict, alcoholic and smoker and died at the age of thirty-seven from complications due to the diabetes. My older sister, Debbie (who was nearly thirteen years older than me), had a child at the age of sixteen, in December 1968. She had to run away so Mom would not force her to have an abortion. Mom and Dad adopted her son Matt, my nephew in 1971 when he was two years old. My sister, Debbie became a prostitute and gave birth to another son. A few years later, she had one more son. All her sons were taken from her due to not being able to take care of them. She was an alcoholic and drug addict. She died at the age of sixty-one due to complications due to diverticulitis.

My brother Bruce was supposed to be the "Golden Child." Everyone adored him. He had a great machinist job and had a home of his own. However, he became an alcoholic and drug addict, and four months after losing my sister, my brother was found dead at a Honolulu, Hawaii halfway house he was living in, in February 2014. He was sixty years old.

Basically, with the examples around me and my extensive traumatic experiences, I had a pathway set up for me to beliving on welfare, to die early or to be a drug addict or alcoholic. Instead, I used my running as my weapon. Against the odds, I graduated from high school, enlisted in the Air Force, graduated from a four-year college, owned my own company, and enlisted in the Oregon Army National Army, where I was mobilized to the Middle East as a Photojournalist. During my difficult childhood, I ran. I ran when I was mad. I ran when I was glad. I ran to get high. I ran to get strong. I ran to make others see me as a good person. I ran to get first. I ran when I got older. It was my savior and it guided me. Running saved my life.

CHAPTER EIGHT

Style and flair – the unique personality of a vibrant man

Dickie is not only known for his running and athletic prowess, (and many other things, of course!), but for his unique style and presence. This is a characteristic of Dickie which goes way back—at least to 1968 and his green sport coat. Dickie wrote an article in the *Terre Haute Tribune* on Friday, the 19th of January, 1968 that highlighted his sense of style, and his understanding of the importance of the visual impression you can make.

"Some of you people," he wrote (as Sullivan Basketball Coach, in Sullivan Indiana), might be wondering why I have traded my blazer coat with the Sullivan patch for a new sport coat. My basketball team gave me a gift certificate for Christmas and with a little from my pocket, I purchased my new green plaid sport coat.

"I now wear this coat at every game because it means a great deal to me. You might say it symbolizes togetherness or mutual respect that my team and myself have for each other. It was a very thoughtful gesture on the part of my boys, and I felt that the least I could do to show my appreciation, was to purchase and wear something they could see. The coat means a lot to me and always will, as it stands as a constant reminder of the great group of young men I was associated with this year."[31]

Dickie was also known as "The coach with the Red Socks," a memory noted by Chuck E. Ledbetter Sr. in his article "The Mentor with the Red Socks."[32] Chuck writes, in his chapter about Dickie, who was coach from 1966–1967, that he "vividly recalls what an excellent communicator he was." He

---

[31] Richard Longo, Sullivan Basketball Coach, in *Terre Haute Tribune*, Jan 19, 1968. https://www.loc.gov/item/sn86058048/

[32] Chuck E. Ledbetter, Sr. 2012, in 'Charlestown high School's 'Pirates of the Hardwood,' Chicago Spectrum Press, Louisville, Kentucky, USA.

noted that there were "never any visible signs of frustration from this youthful looking, well-dressed coach when he took his team to the hardwood (gym floor). He always provided positive analysis of his team's performance, never gave excuses for his team's losses, but calmly presented it as a new challenge in teaching the skills of the game."Lonnie Biggers, quoted in the chapter, described Dickie in glowing terms too. "He wanted you to have fun playing the game of basketball;he would set you down before practice and explain what he wanted out of you. He knew basketball and could get the best out of you. He knew you better than you knew yourself. Longo should have been a psychologist! He was a good mentor."[33]

Dickie's friend Lori Gaston is one person who has been inspired by Dickie and wrote on behalf of the New Orleans Track Club, as a newly elected member of the Board of Directors.

Lori described Dickie as "my friend and one of the coolest cats in the running community of New Orleans and surrounding regions." Lori found Dickie on the road "many years ago," at a New Orleans Track Club race in 2013. She described him as "the spiffiest runner for sure in his colorful shorts and T-shirt," having run with him at NOTC's Greek Fest 5k, where his unique style had shone and caught her attention. She remembered his speed and his smile, and the way he greeted many of the racers on the course.

New to running road races, Lori remembers seeing him race that day and thinking to herself that if this man could put himself out there in that "not so sweet summer sweat," so could she. Dickie is described by Lori and "a source of positivity" and a "hero" and she gives him credit for helping her become a better runner, as she watched him climb podiums to collect his medals, trophies and prizes. To Lori, Dickie represents the motto, "No guts, no glory" and she believes he is living proof of this motto in his running life.

Lori was honored to present Dickie with a New Orleans Track Club Spirit Award at the January 2020 club member meeting. Lori has not had an easy life, having been diagnosed in April 2018 with lung failure, pneumonia, and more than twelve blood clots. Returning to health, she ran one of her first races in summer 2018 pacing just behind Dickie and followed his bright shorts. She stated, "I was scared, I was nervous, I felt better running behind him. He made me feel like everything would be all right. It was."

---

[33] Ledbetter, as above, pg. 136.

Dickie likes to wear bright clothes when he is racing and takes pride in standing out on the field. Some of his running "uniforms," include a combination of bright yellow shorts with a light blue shirt and light blue shoes and another of bright orange shorts with an orange shirt and orange shoes. Dickie likes to kid people that he is sometimes mistaken for a traffic cone in his all-orange outfit. A few other favorite selections include the following—a pair of lime green shorts with a dark blue shirt and green shoes, a lime-green, long sleeve shirt, dark blue shorts and dark blue shoes and a bright yellow shirt, red shorts, and red shoes! It's all about the colors! Dickie's running shoe collection is a veritable rainbow, currently spanning white, dark blue, yellow, and light blue, orange, red and light blue, and every day he will choose a different pair to train in.

Dickie recalls that when he was a teenager, he had one pair of jeans (which were called Levi's at the time) which would be worn all week and handwashed on Sundays. He was invited to a party of one of the girls he knew, who was quite well off, and politely refused the invitation, as tempting as it was, stating that he had to take care of his brother Bob. It was not true, of course, the truth was that Dickie did not have any clothes to wear to the party. Fortunately, those days are certainly in the past and he is now the proud owner of eight suits, ten sports coats, many dress shirts, thirty ties and pocket handkerchiefs, and he "dresses like a million bucks!" Speaking of sports coats, Dickie has a great story about one. He told it like this:

"My wife had a cousin who was ninety-eight. We went to visit him in his home, and he told us he was moving into an assisted living facility and was getting rid of most of his clothes. We were about the same size, so he told me to go to the closet and pick out anything I wanted. I picked out an old Madre sports coats in an Indian pattern with multicolors. The cousin said that this coat was at least fifty-eight years old, but it looked like new. I still wear that coat to church two to three times a year, and people love it." Dickie has many photos taken of him in the coat and he is always reminded of Beverley's cousin when he wears it, a man who Dickie describes as "a great man who I loved dearly, and a very fit man who walked very day and lived to a good age of one hundred and one."

Dickie reflects on the styles of running outfits and noted that they have changed a lot since he started running seventy-three years ago. In those days, running pants were short with slits up each side and in basic colors of black, grey, and brown and all runners wore undershirts. Most of the shorts were black and the shirts white. These then evolved into slightly longer shorts with no slits, mostly in black but now introducing grey and brown. T-shirts evolved into spandex which was form-fitting and usually in black, though sometimes multicolors are seen. In winter runners tend to wear tight warmup outfits, and Dickie can be found proudly decked out in bright orange warmup pants and the blue warmup jacket he won at a state championship 5k race.

With his confidence in dressing to impress, it is probably not going to come as a surprise that Dickie has had fun wearing costumes, too, and has at various times entered many of the themed races run by the track club, fully embracing the invitation to dress outlandishly. In a recent 5k race he was seen in a pink tutu, which he jokingly referred to as "a bad sight!" It is not only in recent years, either, that he's been seen in costume.

In 1964, Dickie took the head basketball coaching position in a nice high school, where there were four other young coaches. The rock band/singing group The Beatles from England were taking the US by storm. Dickie and three other coaches decided to enter the high school annual talent show, wearing floppy hair wigs, suits and "playing" instruments from the band department, and their act was a lip sync of six Beatles songs. Dickie played Paul McCartney, and the group were a big hit because of the popularity of the band at the time, even lining up after the show to sign autographs! He recalls the occasion with joy, describing it as "a really fun time some fifty years ago."

In 1960, when Dickie was in college and playing on the basketball team, Dickie displayed his sense of humor and cheekiness in a way that nearly got him in trouble. According to him, his college had the best team the school had in years, and after winning their conference they were invited to play for the small college national championship. At the time, the other students were very indifferent about the basketball team's accomplishment and they wanted to bring a little attention to what they had done.

Dickie, known for his innovative ideas, was invited to think up a scheme. Hilariously, and rather cheekily, he decided to lead the team in a "panty-raid," where the boys stormed through the girls dorm, yelling "panty-raid," and girls were throwing their panties out of the doors left, right, and other male students joined in. Finally, the furor was stopped when someone called the security alarm, and the boys ran for their lives. Dickie escaped, but he did not get away from his girlfriend's admonition! As Dickie himself put it, "how running saves lives, one pair of panties at a time!"

Running story eight – Jane Brown

Running for me started as my role as "family gear monitor." Each year my family would get together on Veterans Day weekend at our summer cottage in the Outer Banks of North Carolina for the Southern Fried Half Marathon. It was a role I enjoyed in the early years of retirement. About five years in, my new daughter-in-law suggested I run the following year. I was pleased she thought that I could join the group, as it appeared that my fitness routine and classes were paying off!My sister-in-law joined the conversation, suggesting the Jeff Galloway method of walk/run intervals. The pieces started to fit together and five years later after many races, I came one week short of competing in the Shamrock Marathon in Virginia Beach, Virginia (due to the COVID-19 pandemic)

My running journey has taken me from setting off the high blood pressure alarm to being fully prepared to complete my first full marathon, with the love of my life at my side.

My journey shows how running saves lives, one runner at a time, just as Dickie reminds us in his wonderful stories.

The Longo Scholarship Fund and Vision

After many months of frustration, with races cancelled, Dickie's recent post on Facebook (23rd January 2021), demonstrates both his continuing drive to run and the progress of his Longo Scholarship Fund.

Dickie wrote: "Ran my first race in a month today. Great weather, sixty degrees. About two hundred and ninety runners in the race. Masks unless running. More female runners than males. This is the norm in today's races. Males run to win their age group whereas females run to win but also for other reasons such as weight control, socialization, find new running friends, run with a group,and other reasons that are all good. Males should run for those same reasons.

"Had the privilege of giving away twenty-pairs of shoes. Runners really showed their appreciation.Won the 80+, and was 3rd in 70+. Average time for me at 33:56.

Get this award, a five-pound bag of Dole Pineapple Chunks, and a nice trivet. Great award. Wife is going to make a fruit salad with main ingredient being… yes, pineapple.

Hard week of training for a race on Saturday over bridge and back. Tough. Can't wait.Stay safe my wonderful friends. Love to all."

Dickie's vision for his Longo Scholarship Fund was born from his natural inclination to give. Initially he was drawing from his own savings to give away running shoes, running outfits, money and race entry fees to needy runners and homeless veterans, and then he decided to return to work, spending his pay on helping others. He was also giving away money for other needs, for example, to buy a used car for a young lady in need, seven hundred dollars for a funeral of his wife's friend, three hundred dollars for a musical instrument for a needy student and two hundred dollars for school tuition for a student in

Ethiopia. Other examples of giving included cash to a newly unemployed young lady, one hundred dollars to a man from Haiti after an earthquake, and regular payments to various needy people.

As his giving grew, he decided he needed to establish a more formal fund account to handle all of his disbursements—and so was born the Longo Scholarship Fund, which then opened up the fund for contributions from other like-minded philanthropists.

Dickie states that he will dedicate any royalties he receives for this book, once other costs are paid, into the Fund, with his mission to "help as many people as I can with whatever time I have left on this earth."

"I think the happiest people in the world are runners," he writes, when describing his mission and the Longo Scholarship Fund. "I feel they are happy because running keeps them healthy. A lot of socialization takes place in races and in running clubs. I do not think I know an unhappy runner except when they suffer an injury (which is only natural, and usually overcome by a will to get back on the track as quickly as possible)."

In the writing of this book, I hope that Dickie's dream of helping those in need, particularly those who want to share in his beloved sport of running, benefit widely—and that you, as a reader, have found Dickie's story an inspiration in some way. As I have come to know Dickie, from across the other side of the world in Australia, his story and his Facebook posts have been incredibly motivating to me, so much so that I am now training for my first marathon at the end of the year. A positive drive, kindness and optimism are some of the most wonderful qualities a person can have, and the best thing about them is that they are contagious, and unlike COVID-19, we are certainly not seeking a vaccine against them.

I would like to thank anyone who has contributed to this book. This includes:

> Dickie Longo—the man with a mission! It has been a joy getting to know you and I am very thankful you have trusted me to get your story into a book form.

> Dickie's three sons and his great-niece Kayla Longo, who have kindly contributed their stories about Dickie to this book.

To Agatha Kerr, who donated her time to proofread the manuscript and Donna Pazdera, who went over and above to interview Dickie and posted the interview on her Podcast.

My partner Jason, who loves running and faithfully pounded the track beside me when I ran my first half marathon and continues to encourage me as we train together for our first marathons.

My three children, who inspire me to be the best version of myself, as their role model.

The generous friends and readers who have contributed their running stories to this book and their time to encouraging Dickie in his endeavours on his Facebook posts. You are all amazing.

Stats

- As of this writing: Age 84
- Won 426 races in 25 years of competitive racing.
- Goal is to win 500 races by age 88.
- Ranked in the top 2,090 in USA and top 3,090 in World for 5k race in 80+ age division.
- Won 250 tennis tournaments in 40 years of competitive tournaments.
- Have a running streak of 3,860 days.
- Have given away 70 pairs of runnings shoes in past 3 years, more to come. This through the Longo Scholarship fund.

How my dog saved my life. I have suffered a ruptured Achilles tendon injury and had surgery to repair it. Before the injury I would go running with my wonderful golden retriever, Miss Ginger. Every day about 4:00 she would go stand by the front door and paw it and wag her tail telling me it was time for us to go running.

After the surgery I asked the doctor if I could ever run again. He said no, do something else. Didn't want to do anything else so just sat on the couch. Every day Miss Ginger would go to door at 4:00 and paw it wanting to go for a run. I would just tell her can't go running. Finally one day I just said I can't keep letting her down so I put on my running shoes for the first time in 5 months. We went out of the door and did a short 2 mile run and she wagged her tail the whole way.

I really feel she saved my life by getting me off of the couch and running with her. Now at age 84 I run everyday and a race every weekend. Had I not started running again I feel I would be gone by now. Thanks to my great Miss Ginger I am still here.

I finally got a date with the prettiest girl I have ever seen. We were in college and I had asked her for a date the day I saw her at the freshman orientation session. She said no because she was going steady with a boy back home. Sophomore year I asked her for a date and she said no way. Junior year I did the same with same result. About the start of senior year a friend of hers asked me if I still wanted a date with her. I said yes and the friend said I should ask her now. I did so and she said yes. Halaylo.

Dated steadily for awhile and then I asked her to wear my fraternity pin hooked to hers. Back then in 1960 this was a form of being engaged.

It was tradition at my college that when a frat brother pinned a girl he got thrown into the school pond that had been filled with food coloring.

I heard that the frat brothers were coming after me to catch me and throw me in pond. I took off running and no one could catch me. They all tired out while I was still going strong. Another example of how running saves lives. That beautiful girl and I have been going steady for 61 years.

Went to a race and upon arriving I had to go to the bathroom as all of us runners have to do. I had driven 70 miles to get to race so a bathroom visit was awaiting me.

There were no port a lets only a single indoor bathroom. Entered the bathroom and a sign on door said "out of order". I was frantic because I had to do number 2. Went back out to my car and picked up my small roll of toilet paper that I keep in car for emergencies.

Run down sidewalk a little ways and ducked into wooded area. Found a place and started to do my business. Heard a rushing real close to me and thought it might be an animal. Much to my surprise it was a runner doing his business also. Heard him rushing around trying to find some leaves. I asked him if he needed some toilet paper. He said you have saved my life. Threw him the roll and we both run the race with no problems.

How running saves lives one roll at a time.

I had taken my SUV to get oil changed. I then ran about a mile to a big park that had a two mile oval around it. I ran around the oval and then sat down on a bench near water fountain. There was a man sitting next to me with his shoes off. I look down at his shoes and could not believe my eyes. The worst pair of walking/running shoes I have seen. Big cuts along each side. No laces. Heel area turned flat.Shoes completely broken down. I asked him if he ran in those shoes. He said no they keep coming off. Only walk. Noticed top of his feet were red from sunburn.

I asked him if he would be here tomorrow at 4:00 PM   like he was today. He said yes. I then asked his shoe size. Said 11. Be here tomorrow. He said Si.

Next day I got to the park at 4:00 and he was waiting for me. Gave him a nice pair of Hoka shoes, 3 running shirts, 2 pair of running socks, and two $20 bills. He started to tear up so I headed out to parking lot.

Got in SUV and was pulling out of parking lot and noticed he had started running. That brought a tear to my eyes.

How running saves lives one old pair and one new pair of shoes at a time.

Had taken my SUV to get ties rotated. I always go for a run while waiting for them to do the tires. It was about 95 degrees in bright sunshine. Ran for an hour and got back to shop. I had become friends with the lady that owns the shop as she handles all my car issues.

I run up to the door and she was standing there with the keys for me. I was feeling a little full of myself for running for an hour in blazing sun. I said to her "I am the toughest 84 yr old you know". She replayed back, " you are the only 84 yr old I know". She sure put me in my place. Humbled.

What is in a name.

When I was head basketball coach at Tulane University I was often ask to speak to various organizations and at many school basketball banquets at the end of the basketball season.

I got a call from the minister of a large church asking me to speak at their basketball banquet. The church had their own youth basketball league.

Of course I said I would be happy to speak to his group.

I got to banquet room and a lady came up to me and said she was going to introduce me. She asked how to pronounce my name. I said LONGO.

I said easy way to remember it is that it is the opposite of SHORTSHOP. Longo - Shortstop.

She got up to podium and said, " Here is Tulane basketball coach, Coach Shortstop."

Everyone laughed. I didn't even correct her but went right into my presentation.

Noticed looking around at the group getting ready to run a 5k race a young couple and their baby daughter in a stroller. Love to see families running together with their children.

After the race I made it a point to talk to them and to tell them how much I admired them running the race as a family.

As I usually do I asked them when will they run another race. Dad said we run 2 races a year. Said entry fee too much and baby stroller not good to run in.

Told them to wait here a few minutes. Went to my car and wrote out check for $500 and ran back to them. I said this check will allow you to run more races and pay on a running stroller. They couldn't believe it. A complete stranger giving them money to continue their running endeavors. Mom gave me big hug. Dad a big thanks.

This from the Longo Scholarship Fund design to help others.

How running saves lives one stroller at a time.

Went for my daily 4 mile run down the sidewalk of a very busy street that had a stop light at almost every crossing. Came up to red stop light and stopped for turning traffic. A junk of a car pulled up and stopped next to me . It was dented, smoke pouring out from somewhere and in terrible shape. I had a wrap on my leg where I had ruptured Achilles tendon surgery. A young man holler at me " bad leg old man, get off the street." Continue running down street and had to stop at next light. Junk car sitting at the light. I run up to junker and said " I am in better shape than that piece of junk you are in."

Light changed and man threw some coins at me hitting me in chest and legs.

They just took off with smoke pouring into the air. Pollution.

Such are the perils of running on busy street.

When we runners get together and talk, what are the most important words we can say to each other?

5 most important words are: "I am proud of you"

4 most important words are: "What is your opinion "

3 most important words are: "If you please"

2 most important words are: " Thank you"

The least important word is "I"

Be a good listener and not a good talker. You learn from listening.

Was at a race recently and a young lady runner and a friend came up to me to ask me something. The runner said she was not racing today but came with her friend and this was going to be her first 5k race ever. She said she had been in a few races with me and would I do the following. I said what?

She said could her friend run with me in the race. Said her friend knows nothing about pace or timing. I of course agreed to let her run with me.

We were running together and she was almost glued to my hip. Stayed right with me all the way until we could see the finish line. I told her to take off and finish fast. Boy, did she take off. Great finish. I was a little ways behind her.

At the finish line she was waiting for me and gave me a big hug. Nice.

They gave out the age group awards and as I always do I won the 80+.

To her amazement she got 2nd in her age group.

Told her next race she is capable of picking up her pace quite a bit. Said I had faith in her and she would win her age group. She said thanks with big smile on her face.

A lifetime runner in the making.

A small group of us runners were talking together before the pending race we were about to run. We were talking about winning and loosing races. A young lady kind of asked me if I prayed to win since I seem to win my age group all the time.

My reply is that I did not pray to win. No. I always say a short prayer to keep me safe and ask God to give me the ability to run to my potential.

My potential might be good enough to win. Then again the other runner's potential might be greater than mine and he wins. I just ask God help me use my ability to the fullest. Win or lose I have reached my potential. Amen.

12 TERRE HAUTE TRIBUNE. Friday, Jan. 19, '68

Explains New Coat

By RICHARD LONGO
Sullivan Basketball Coach

SULLIVAN, Ind. — Some of you people might be wondering why I have traded my blazer coat with the Sullivan patch for a new sport coat. My basketball team gave me a gift certificate for Christmas and with a little from my pocket, I purchased my new green plaid sport coat.

I now wear this coat at every game because it means a great deal to me. You might say it symbolizes togetherness or mutual respect that my team and myself have for each other.

It was a very thoughtful gesture on the part of my boys and I felt the least I could do to show my appreciation was to purchase and wear something they could see. The coat means a lot to me and always will, as it stands as a constant reminder of the great group of young men I was associated with this year.

Three Losses—Gain Knowledge

The combined record of the teams that have inflicted losses on my Arrows in 1968 is 31-8. South Knox owns a 12-2 record and beat us by 4 at South Knox. North Central's slate reads 11-2 and they beat us by 2 in an overtime.

Garfield, which leads the WIC with a 5-0 record, owns an overall 8-4 record and they beat us by 20 at Garfield. I offer all the above facts to indicate that we are playing some of the better teams, record-wise, in the area.

Having lost to all three is quite disheartening, but nevertheless, we have gained a great deal of basketball knowledge on which we are building basketball heritage at Sullivan.

These three teams are definitely basketball schools and have a lot of rich basketball background to carry them over teams like us. Sullivan, being a football school (and I get awful tired of people using this an an excuse) cannot reach back to heritage and win the close one because there is no heritage there.

Coach Don McDonald of Garfield said that their great basketball heritage has really helped them win games this year. And I am sure Paul Weekly of North Central and Alford of South Knox can ditto McDonald's statement.

Creatures of Habit

The human being is definitely a creature of habit and Sullivan possesses no habit of winning. I feel the greatest thing that I as the Sullivan coach is faced with is the non-winning attitude my boys possessed at the start of the season.

Some of my team members have never played on a winning team in their lives. Others played on a winning team in Jr. High, but their schedule then did not include any of the tough Terre Haute schools that my varsity must battle now.

Fundamentals are grossly important; defense is vital; shooting must be mastered; but without the winning attitude, all the other aspects are in vain.

We must become the creature of habit in that we mentally gear ourselves toward the positive goal of winning every time we take the floor. If we possessed the winning habit, I dare say we could of beaten South Knox, North Central and Garfield.

It is my job to teach my boys fundamentals that are lacking and all the other skills it takes to compete successfully. However, it is of vital importance to instill within my boys the habit of winning.

First Losing Season ? ?

With a 3-8 record and only nine games left on our cshedule, I am almost assured my first losing season in my coaching career. I have experienced seven winning seasons since I first entered the coaching ranks in 1960.

Any intelligent individual would safely assume that we cannot and will not break even for the year. However, I must be the dumbest guy around because I feel we can do just that —break even.

I have confidence that my Arrows can win seven of their nine remaining games to produce an even season. I can see marked improvement in each of our last three games, and once we get that winning attitude, we can start knocking them off one by one.

With the likes of Brazil and North Knox on the road and powerful Clinton at home, we have our work cut out for us. But, I know these boys want to produce the first even season in five years and they can do it. You good fans must be commended for your great support at Garfield on a very dangerous night last Friday. Please don't give up on these boys yet I still believe they will come through for you.

Richard Longo, 1968, Article 'Explains new Coat'.

The Coaches Corner

By Dick Longo

BACK GLANCING

Well, this column will go to press before we play another game, so I want to use this space to do a little back glancing. I arrived in Charlestown in mid-August last summer and was greeted with the chant, "it's really going to be a rough year for you", or "you can't win many games this year", or "I've never seen Charlestown so low on talent."

I realize people were trying to sort of condition me to the situation and also they were predicting our success for the season. Well, we went to work on Oct. 1 and won a few more games than was expected in the early part of the season. We beat Crothersville, as expected, and lost to Silver Creek and Paoli. For the next 6 games we split just about each week, either winning or losing every other Friday.

The Christmas Tournament found us playing very well, over our heads, in losing to Silver Creek by 4 and bombing Clarksville by 21 points. Since the Tourney we have been playing the kind of ball everyone predicted for us to play in that we have won 2 and lost 4.

Since 1966 was ushered in, we have played the type of ball we are capable of. Through sheer fight and determination we won 6 games in 1965 and played a little over our heads. Now, we have come back to earth and are preforming at our level of capability.

SECTIONAL WARM-UP

The thing we have to work to obtain is the level of play we were experiencing early in the season. Every team experiences a "slump" sometime during the year, and we feel ours is over now that we lost 2 games on successive nights.

With the Sectional tournament just two weeks away, we have to polish our offensive attack, decide what type of defense we want to employ, and prepare ourselves mentally for the big show.

The team that is in good shape physically, and most of all mentally, will win the Madison Sectional. The host school Madison is famous for being mentally "up" and ready for the Sectional. If another team with like talent could get themselves "up" mentally, the 9 year reign Madison holds could be broken. As I see it, there are 4 teams who might pull the big upset in the Sectional.

Vevay has great speed and shooting ability, but their biggest problem will be rebounding with the large squads.

New Washington has great shooters and rebounding strength, and their problem might be their lack of speed in their under men. However, the likes of Charlie Stewart and Dennis Jones can carry a team a long way.

Southwestern has good rebounding strength and good shooters, but once again a lack of speed might hurt the charges of coach Stan Weber.

I am analyzing these teams in the light of what they would need to upset Madison, the tournament favorites.

As far as projecting my own ball club into the upset role, I can say that its bad to go too far out on a limb because when you do, someone cuts it off. I feel we have played well enough at times to beat a good team like Madison, but not lately.

We have average speed, average rebounding ability, just a little below average shooting ability, (hitting just 36% for season as a team), and average intelligence.

I do feel, however, we have good defensive ability and knowledge. If we can get supreme rebounding efforts from Lon Biggers, Tony Glotzbach, Roger Adams, and John Boyd, we could be above average on the boards. If we can get good team defense and control the game to our style of play, we could be tough.

It's going to take hard-nose defense for us to spring the big upset because we have found we can't rely on hot shooting to carry us. This hot shooting spree is not a continuous thing with us, it runs in spurts, so we must win by out-defensing our opponent and controlling the boards. I'll promise one thing, we'll fight hard to make you fans proud of us, win or lose.

STATISTICS --

Dick Longo, 1962-1965, Charleston H.S. Basketball Coach,
First coach to have his own newspaper column.

Thursday, November 11, 1965

Accent On Sports

by Charlie Jenkins

PIRATES GIVE GOOD ACCOUNTING

The pessimist feeling that the Charlestown fans might see their favorites suffer through a long season was partially wiped away last Friday night at the Silver Creek gym in Sellersburg.

True, the Pirates didn't win. In fact, they lost by 15 points. But still the play of the Bucs brought rays of sunshine both to head mentor Dick Longo and Pirate fans.

As Longo himself said, "I don't mind losing if you can learn from losing. I think we learned two or three things that will help us." Those according to the coach were "aggressiveness, blocking out rebounding, and getting the good shot a little bit better."

Longo, the man in the red socks, saw his club play the highly-thought-of Dragons tooth and nail until they wore down in the last five minutes. One of the turning points in the game, said the coach, was the fouling out of center Tony Glotzbach with a little more than seven minutes to go. The slender 6-3 pivotman fought the boards pretty well against the likes of Silver Creek's big three of Reid Bailey, David Lewis and Art Beck. As Longo remarked, "that took about half of our rebounding strength away."

The failure of veteran Lonnie Biggers to get started in the second half was another determining factor. Charlestown trailed only 34-28 at halftime and Biggers had nine points. But in the second half, the 5-10 senior was held scoreless and most of all, as Longo put it, "Biggers' walking so much hurt us a great deal, too."

Longo went on, "In the second half he missed his last 14 shots and he walked a great deal. That's not like Lonnie."

The coach was "real pleased with my guard play." He had words of praise both for "traffic cop" Ben Ledbetter and Bill Somerville. Longo called Ledbetter, who chipped in with 14 points to tie Pepper Cooper for high point honors, "a good heady ballplayer." Of Somerville, who scored 9 points and moved well, Longo said, "He's probably our quickest boy."

The coach, on our "Meet the Coach" show last Saturday, summed up the loss this way, "We played pretty well at times. We fought with 'em. But you must look at it in this respect, our defense wasn't geared enough at this time of the year to stop the likes of Bailey, Lewis and some of these other boys that they have that are tremendous shooters."

But Longo added, "I'd be glad to play them again in the future, because I think we can show up a little bit better." He says he wouldn't mind drawing them in the first game of the holiday tourney at Silver Creek.

PAOLI NEXT

Paoli's crackerbox gym is the next visiting spot for the traveling Pirates. One consolation is the fact that Gary Holland, one of Southern Indiana's better players, is gone. He's now on an athletic scholarship at University of Louisville.

But coach Mike Gooding still returns three good men in 6-3 center George Mikels, 5-10 guard Trent Magner and Vincent Vance, a chunky 6-0, 175 pound forward.

While the Pirates didn't have much trouble subduing the Rams last season, some of the other clubs had a "night of horror" in the crackerbox at Paoli.

Sectional champion Providence played one of its better games, but still lost 100-96 and Silver Creek was bowled over 115 to 96.

Those scores give you an idea of how the Rams know every nook and cranny in the ancient structure.

Jenkins, Charlie_1965, 'Accent on Sports' article about Dickie Longo.

Dickie and Bob – younger years

45th anniversary June 25, 2005 – Dickie and Beverley
Sons, Rob, Ross, Reed

A4 Profile Tulane Basketball Coach age 32

Beverley 1968

Coach Longo pic Charlestown 1966 – 1967
Won Basketball Tournament

Dickie and Bob with Bikes for Christmas

Dickie and Beverley June 1954

Dickie and brother Bob at Ross's Wedding 25th Dec 2012

Dickie and son Reed May 2006

Dickie in suit 27th April 2011

Dickie in suit unknown date

The fire of competition still burns brightly in Dick Longo's heart

Dick Longo '60 has embraced the competitive nature of sports since his high school and college days as a varsity athlete in football, baseball, basketball, and track, and in later years as a high school and college head coach.

At age 75, he's still at it, keeping in shape through running while winning championships in tennis tournaments on a regular basis. He leaves no doubt as to why he continues his rigorous regimen at an age when many might prefer to simply take life a little more easily.

"The competition is what brings me to it," he said. "The only place I can be competitive anymore is on the tennis court."

Longo, who lives in Metairie, La., a suburb of New Orleans, is currently ranked No. 2 in Louisiana in the 75-80 age group by the United States Tennis Association, but was No. 1 for more than 20 years before a newcomer from Texas came in last year. He has been ranked as high as No. 12 in the South and has won 285 tournaments so far. His goal is 500 wins. He has won the state Senior Olympics tennis championship in his age group for 20 straight years.

Longo was introduced to tennis through intramurals at Transylvania, where he was a varsity baseball and basketball player under former head coach C. M. Newton. Other than that, he is a self-taught player who relies on his conditioning and ability to keep the ball in play to defeat his opponents. He plays singles exclusively, disdaining the less demanding doubles popular with many seniors.

"I used to come to the net all the time in my younger days, but now I stay mostly on the baseline," he said. "I'm a counter-puncher—I keep the ball in play as long as I can. I figure if I can get the ball over the net one more time, my opponent's going to make a mistake. One of my better lob shots is to the backhand corner—if I can get him on his heels back there, then I'll come to the net."

Longo was a high school basketball coach in Kentucky and Indiana before becoming assistant basketball coach at Tulane University in the late 1960s. He was head coach at Tulane for three years before leaving coaching to become a sales representative for Houghton-Mifflin-Harcourt in their textbook lines, a position he still holds.

Longo grew up in Ft. Lauderdale, Fla., and was a high school senior when Newton, a native of Ft. Lauderdale, recruited him to come to Transylvania.

"One day C. M. called and said, 'I'm going to come by and pick you up in my station wagon and take you up to Transylvania and you're going to play ball for me.' I had an offer from Florida State University to play football, but it was an all-men's school at the time.

"I'm so glad C. M. recruited me. I loved my days at Transylvania, where I met my lovely wife (**Beverly Jouett Longo '60**). If it weren't for Transylvania, I wouldn't be happily married for 52 years now. It has a dear place in my heart."

Dickie Longo article age 75

June 2003 National Senior Olympics Tennis

Longo Family Christmas Card 2016

Mother, Dickie and Bob before she left

GETS POST — Richard Longo, 32, has been named assistant basketball coach at Tulane University. A graduate of Transylvania College, he is married to the former Beverley Jouett, daughter of Ed Jouett, Winchester. Longo formerly served as assistant basketball coach at Shelbyville, head coach at Harrodsburg and is presently head coach at Sullivan (Ind.) High School. The Longos will move to New Orleans Aug. 1. In addition to coaching, Longo also will teach a class in physical education and recruit basketball players.

Newspaper Article Aged 32 Basketball assistant coach Tulane uni

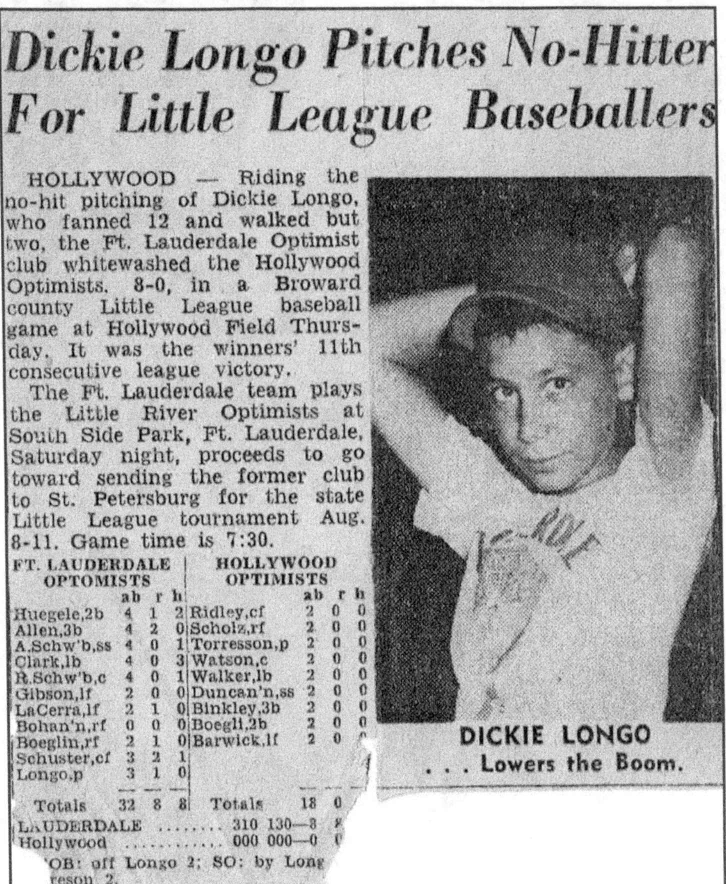

Dickie Longo Pitches No-Hitter For Little League Baseballers

HOLLYWOOD — Riding the no-hit pitching of Dickie Longo, who fanned 12 and walked but two, the Ft. Lauderdale Optimist club whitewashed the Hollywood Optimists. 8-0, in a Broward county Little League baseball game at Hollywood Field Thursday. It was the winners' 11th consecutive league victory.

The Ft. Lauderdale team plays the Little River Optimists at South Side Park, Ft. Lauderdale, Saturday night, proceeds to go toward sending the former club to St. Petersburg for the state Little League tournament Aug. 8-11. Game time is 7:30.

FT. LAUDERDALE OPTOMISTS	ab	r	h	HOLLYWOOD OPTIMISTS	ab	r	h
Huegele,2b	4	1	2	Ridley,cf	2	0	0
Allen,3b	4	2	0	Scholz,rf	2	0	0
A.Schw'b,ss	4	0	1	Torresson,p	2	0	0
Clark,1b	4	0	3	Watson,c	2	0	0
R.Schw'b,c	4	0	1	Walker,1b	2	0	0
Gibson,lf	2	0	0	Duncan'n,ss	2	0	0
LaCerra,lf	2	1	0	Binkley,3b	2	0	0
Bohan'n,rf	0	0	0	Boegli,2b	2	0	0
Boeglin,rf	2	1	0	Barwick,lf	2	0	0
Schuster,cf	3	2	1				
Longo,p	3	1	0				
Totals	32	8	8	Totals	18	0	

LAUDERDALE .... 310 130—8
Hollywood .... 000 000—0

OB: off Longo 2; SO: by Long reson 2,

DICKIE LONGO

. . . Lowers the Boom.

Newspaper clip Dickie Longo pitches No-Hitter for Little League

Ole Man River Half Marathon Nov 3 1996